FEMINISM AND SPORTING BODIES

ESSAYS ON THEORY AND PRACTICE

M. Ann Hall, PhD
University of Alberta

Library of Congress Cataloging-in-Publication Data

Hall, M. Ann (Margaret Ann), 1942-
    Feminism and sporting bodies : essays on theory and practice / M.
Ann Hall.
        p. cm.
    Includes bibliographical references and index.
    ISBN 0-87322-969-X
    1. Sports for women.   2. Feminist theory.   3. Sports--Sex
differences.   4. Sports--Sociological aspects.   I. Title.
GV709.H32   1996   95-44480
796'.0194--dc20   CIP

ISBN: 0-87322-969-X

Acquisitions Editor: Rick Frey, PhD; **Developmental Editor:** Julie Rhoda; **Assistant Editors:** Susan Moore, Kirby Mittelmeier, Chad Johnson, and Sandra Merz Bott; **Editorial Assistants:** Andrew T. Starr and Jennifer J. Hemphill; **Copyeditor:** Heather Shupp; **Proofreader:** Kathy Bennett; **Indexer:** Barbara E. Cohen; **Typsetter and Layout Artist:** Yvonne Winsor; **Text Designer:** Judy Henderson; **Cover Designer:** Jack Davis; **Printer:** Versa Press

Printed in the United States of America   10   9   8   7   6   5   4   3   2   1

Human Kinetics
P.O. Box 5076, Champaign, IL 61825-5076
1-800-747-4457

Canada: Human Kinetics, Box 24040, Windsor, ON N8Y 4Y9
1-800-465-7301 (in Canada only)

Europe: Human Kinetics, P.O. Box IW14, Leeds LS16 6TR, United Kingdom
(44) 1132 781708

Australia: Human Kinetics, 2 Ingrid Street, Clapham 5062, South Australia
(08) 371 3755

New Zealand: Human Kinetics, P.O. Box 105-231, Auckland 1
(09) 523 3462

Contents

Preface

My purpose in *Feminism and Sporting Bodies* is to "speak feminism" to physical educators, sport studies students and scholars, and sportswomen. During the past 25 years there has been an astounding growth of feminist theory, research, and scholarship, and over this same period many of us have contributed to the discourse about gender and sport by consistently and systematically applying a feminist analysis. In some ways this book is an update of *Sport and Gender: A Feminist Perspective on the Sociology of Sport*, my first attempt (in the late 1970s) to bring feminism to the study of sport.

The debates in feminist theory can be bewildering to someone coming to them for the first time. The older feminisms—*liberal, radical, Marxist,* and *socialist*—no longer are adequate to map the terrain of feminist theory. There have been significant conceptual shifts in this theory over the last two decades so that today contemporary feminist approaches also include the *cultural* and the *postmodern*. All of these terms and theoretical positions are defined and elaborated upon in the chapters that follow. My primary purpose is to explain at least some of the debates surrounding these varying positions within feminism and to show their relevance to sport and physical education. *Feminism and Sporting Bodies* provides an entry point for physical educators and others in sport studies who are unfamiliar with feminist research and criticism in sociology, history, and cultural theory. I also hope that women's studies students and scholars already familiar with feminist theory will find something unique in its application to sport and physical education.

It is no longer appropriate to speak of *one* feminism or even to refer to "feminists," as if we were all of one mind. There is a seemingly endless variety of feminisms particularly when we look globally. Whatever its stripe, feminism still must provide a place from which women can speak, make political demands, and challenge patriarchal structures. To apply any particular brand of feminism to the gender and sport discourse is to make it more political. Although the politics and practices of feminism have not always been recognized by sportswomen as important or relevant, my hope is that by reading this book they will understand the need for feminist theory and the relationship between theory and practice.

Although each essay in the book is discrete and can be read on its own, there is a logic to the whole. Chapter 1 recounts my 30-year intellectual odyssey in the struggle to understand and apply feminist theory. Chapter 2 describes how the earlier discourses of "women and sport" moved away from biological and categoric explanations, and why much of this research, which still continues, is of little practical use. It is now more appropriate to speak of "gender relations," which requires a critical analysis of the power relations between the genders and how sport reproduces and perpetuates these relations. Chapters 3 and 4 review the scholarship within feminist cultural studies as it is applied to sport: Chapter 3 examines the need for theory, history, sexual difference, and masculinity, whereas chapter 4 focuses on the relatively new cultural criticism surrounding the *body*. Chapter 5 then examines the notion of *feminist research*, especially as praxis, and how that research can be applied to the sociocultural study of sport. Finally, I argue in chapter 6 that sport is a political site, specifically a location for the resistance and transformation of gender relations.

Acknowledgments

Whether they knew it or not, many colleagues over the years contributed to this book; in fact, there would be no book without their work. For this particular project, there are four individuals whose contributions were specific, insightful, and enormously helpful. They are Anne Flintoff in England, Pat Griffin in the United States, Marg MacNeill in Canada, and Jim McKay in Australia who were asked by the publisher to review the manuscript. At Human Kinetics, I am grateful to Rick Frey for convincing me to do this book (which was not what I had in mind initially) and for having the patience to wait for it. Julie Rhoda, also at Human Kinetics, performed her editorial duties with exceptional skill and tact. The University of Alberta, where I have spent my entire academic career, provided a leave just when I need to get the work finished. Finally, a special thank-you to Jane Haslett who reminds me from time to time, and often without success, that there is more to our lives than work. Yet she willingly read and commented upon the many drafts, and she remains my most influential critic.

Research Odyssey of a Feminist

1

I sometimes ask students to explain when and under what circumstances they decided that they were or were not feminists. After listening to their stories, I tell them mine. The term *feminism* was not part of my vocabulary until I read Betty Friedan's *The Feminine Mystique* in 1965 while completing my after-degree teacher training. I grew up in the 1940s and 1950s, when "feminist" (like "career woman") had become a dirty word. According to Friedan, early feminists had fought for and eventually won the right to vote. They had "destroyed the old image of women, but they could not erase the hostility, the prejudice, the discrimination that still remained" (p. 100). Although her book interested me, I could not identify with her central thesis that white, middle-class, American housewives were lost, incomplete, disappointed, and almost despairing because of "the problem that had no name." At the time, I was in my early 20s, freshly trained, wildly enthusiastic, and about to embark on a career as a high school physical education teacher. It was full speed ahead into the world of work, not marriage and a family. I was smugly confident that I would escape the boredom and despair Friedan described.

After less than a year in my new career, I was shocked at the blatant discrimination and impossible conditions under which I was expected to teach and encourage young girls to acquire an interest in physical activity. The only female physical education teacher at my school, I was working around the clock preparing lessons (in three subject areas), administering an intramural program, coaching all the girls' teams, and teaching my lessons in a small, dingy gym while my three male counterparts took the best facilities and equipment, and lounged about just waiting for me to crack up. My solution at the end of the school year was to leave and return to university. No one ever asked me why I was leaving, but I carried those awful memories with me for a long time; they fueled much of what I did and thought from then on. Now, nearly thirty years have passed since I landed at the University of Alberta to begin graduate work.

At an international conference held a few years after I returned to graduate school I was giving one of my first papers: "The Role of the Safety Bicycle in the Emancipation of Women" (the "safety" bicycle was the first bicycle with rubber tires rather than bone-jarring metal ones). I concluded, rather grandly, that not only did women use the bicycle as a means of defying tradition, but that it was plausible that many reforms in women's rights would not have come about so quickly without the safety bicycle. The paper was a product of my master's thesis, a history of women's sport in Canada prior to the first World War. After my presentation, an American fellow approached me and stated accusingly: "You must be a women's libber." My quizzical expression prompted him to tell me about the women's liberation movement in the United States, and I listened in amazement. It was the late 1960s, and I knew of no such movement in Canada; even if there was one, I was too busy establishing my new career as a university physical education instructor to take notice. At the time, establishing my career meant teaching a variety of sport activities, coaching the women's swim team, administering women's athletics, establishing a new subfield called the "sociology of sport," and trying to figure out how and in what area I would conduct research.

Becoming a Positivist

In 1971 I went to the University of Birmingham in England to do doctoral work, which allowed me space and time to think about feminism again. I read a number of influential books, all published in the early 1970s—specifically Kate Millett's *Sexual Politics*, Germaine Greer's *The Female Eunuch*, Shulamith Firestone's *The Dialectic of Sex*, Eva Figes's *Patriarchal Attitudes*, Robin Morgan's anthology *Sisterhood is Powerful*, Juliet Mitchell's *Woman's Estate*, and Sheila Rowbotham's *Women, Resistance and Revolution* and *Women's Consciousness, Man's World*. These books are now considered among the classics of second-wave feminism in the English-speaking world.[1] I also read

Simone de Beauvoir's *The Second Sex*, which had been published in French in 1949 and in English in 1953. I simply could not get enough of these books, but paradoxically, although I knew beyond question that I was a feminist, I could not relate this extracurricular reading to my doctoral research. How would the researcher and the feminist become one?

To my knowledge, I was the first Canadian to undertake a doctorate in physical education in England. This made me an oddity because the area was not fully recognized in Britain as a legitimate university subject. My degree was earned entirely through research, and I had taken to England a straightforward question: Why do some women make sport and physical activity an important part of their lives and others do not? When I began my doctorate, I had no formal background in either sociology or sport sociology. Along with physical education, my undergraduate training had been in mathematics and statistics; consequently, the natural science model seemed the most appropriate to answer my question. I was interested in the "whys" of women's involvement in sport, or lack of it, and building a causal mathematical model to explain these whys seemed eminently worthwhile and challenging. Moreover our exemplars in the sociology of sport at the time were proponents of the quest for empirically verifiable, formal theory. In the end, I produced a substantial multivariate statistical analysis that "proved," among other things, that the more you liked physical activity and sport when you were younger, the more likely you were to keep doing it when you were older. My dissertation, *Women and Physical Recreation: A Causal Analysis*, certainly lived up to a quote I had placed at the beginning: "Don't be afraid to oversimplify reality. It will always be possible to introduce complexities a few at a time" (Blalock, 1971, p. 196).

I had become, to put it simply, a positivist, or someone who believes that (a) reality consists of what is available to the senses, (b) the natural and social sciences share a common logical and methodological foundation, (c) the goal of social research is to create universal laws of human behaviour, and (d) there is a fundamental distinction between fact and value creating the grounds for an "objective" social science (Hughes, 1980). Unfortunately I had then no clear understanding of the epistemological and methodological foundations of social research and little knowledge of the variety of research methods, including qualitative ones, available to us now. I learned all this on my own, an experience that later prompted me to introduce a course for incoming physical education graduate students on social research applications to leisure and sport, a course I have now taught for over 20 years.

My supervisor at the University of Birmingham was Charles Jenkins, a wonderfully sensitive man. His intellectual interests were amazingly eclectic, and although he supported the positivist turn in my work, he did try to interest me in the work of those at the Centre for Contemporary Cultural Studies: people like Stuart Hall, Paul Willis, and Charles Critcher. The Birmingham Centre, as it became known, was at the forefront of British cultural studies, a difficult to define area in which different disciplines intersect in the study of the cultural aspects of society, sport among them (see chapter 3). However, there was little work on leisure or sport being conducted at the Birmingham Centre in the early 1970s; there were no women and certainly no feminists, although by the end of the decade, feminism had forced a major rethinking of every substantive area of work within cultural studies.

In 1973 Charles Jenkins and I organized a conference at Birmingham on Women and Sport. Our purpose was to explore the relationship between biological and cultural influences on women's sport participation through a series of invited papers. Among others, we invited Paul Willis from the Birmingham Centre, who at the time was working on his dissertation, the often cited *Learning to Labour: How Working Class Kids Get Working Class Jobs*, to give a paper. He and I presented papers during the same session. His was a brilliant and insightful discussion of the role of sport in the reinforcement of common-sense ideologies that assert the superiority of men[2] and of how women collude in these ideological definitions,[2] Mine was a complex multiple regression analysis in which I tried to explain the relationships among all the variables in my dissertation. At one point, I remember displaying a slide with the title: "How to Regress in One Easy Lesson." The irony of all this escaped me at the time.

Researching "Women in Sport"

Upon returning to teaching with my newly earned Ph.D., I knew I was going to continue to research in the area of "women in sport" but I did not know from which disciplinary perspective. Having narrowed down the options to the social sciences, I was uncertain whether I would choose history, sociology, psychology, or social psychology, not that I had much training in any of these disciplines. American sport sociologist Susan Birrell (1988) is absolutely correct when she states, "The decade of the 1970s is marked by unevenness in focus and quality as the field struggled first for identity and then for legitimacy" (p. 463). She goes on to point out that women in sport as an area of study must be seen against a backdrop of other social forces. Certainly significant were changes in physical education, which at the time was transforming itself from a profession into an academic discipline, or more accurately a series of subdisciplines now readily identified as the history of sport, sociology of sport, psychology of sport, and so forth. It was, therefore, logical to develop a multidisciplinary women in sport area. Also of importance was second-wave feminism, which produced today's women's movement and a steady growth in women's sport.

The context of Birrell's observations was the United States, and although Canada has followed the American experience in some areas, it has not in others. Legislative and institutional changes in women's sport in the United States, such as the passage of Title IX in 1972,[3] the formation of the Women's Sports Foundation in 1974, and the expansion of opportunities in sport for girls and women, were only marginally felt in Canada during the 1970s, although 1974 did mark the beginning of federal government involvement in the issues with the organizing of the first National Conference on Women and Sport. On the academic front, since most Canadian physical educators teaching in universities went to the United States for doctoral-level training (I was an exception), they brought back the need to compartmentalize the field into its various subdisciplines, and we all felt the same pressure to create our own research specialties. Mine was to be the vaguely defined area of women in sport.

By the mid-1970s I had become immersed in the Canadian women's movement. My tales from that period are too long to narrate here, but through helping to found, or volunteering in, several feminist organizations like the Alberta Status of Women Action Committee, the Canadian Research Institute for the Advancement of Women, and the Canadian Association for the Advancement of Women and Sport, I gained an invaluable network of feminist colleagues across the country. I interacted with them through committee meetings, board meetings, funding crises, hiring committees, marches, lobbying, and celebrating women's culture with feminist sisters both within and outside academe. My involvement taught me an extremely valuable lesson: As feminists, our theory, politics, and practices are inextricably linked. Those working in academe, whose focus is research and scholarship, must work with those on the front line—be they activists, "femocrats," shelter workers, or volunteers—so that together we are doing critical political work. Through the years, I have continued to help document our progress in changing sex inequality within sport and physical education in Canada and to speak out when necessary.

Moving Beyond the Psychological

Feminist theory, a more sophisticated understanding of sociology, and feminist political work were the major influences on my academic research and scholarship as I undertook the task of helping to shape the sociological study of women in sport. The work in that area during the early 1970s, as Susan Birrell (1988) rightly points out, was dominated by psychological rather than sociological analyses of women's place in sport. In fact, my first research article, published in England, was entitled, "A 'Feminine Woman' and an 'Athletic Woman' as Viewed by Female Participants and Non-Participants in Sport" (M.A. Hall, 1972). Using a semantic differential as an attitude measurement tool, I found that nonparticipants showed considerably more "dissonance" between the two concepts than did participants and that this difference was statistically significant.[4] What was I trying to do? Mindful of the popular and often pejorative image of the female athlete as ''unfeminine,'' I wanted to see if this stereotype prevented some women from taking an active interest in sport and to show that for women who did participate, there was a greater congruence between the two images. My conclusion was naive and demonstrated a minimal understanding of the cultural forces and ideological practices at work:

> The present study does seem to suggest that perhaps participation in sport among women could be increased if the image associated with athletic women were somehow changed, so that it became more congruent with the stereotype associated with feminine women. This would also involve the concomitant change in the feminine image toward a direction more consonant with athleticism. (p. 46)

Again Susan Birrell (1988) hits the proverbial nail on the head with her critique that this early research, mine included, ''relied on methodologically primitive attempts to measure complex psychosocial constructs; conceived of women as not fitting into sport; and by subtly assuming that the problem behind women's low involvement lay within, tended to blame women for their own lack of participation'' (p. 467). The topics in a new course, Psychosocial Aspects of Women in Sport, that I had introduced in my department in the early 1970s, reflected this psychological and individualistic bias. The topics covered in the course were sex differences, sex role behaviour, tomboyism, attitudes toward women athletes, the personality traits of women athletes, fear of success, role conflict, psychological androgyny, the apologetic, and socialization. However, any understanding that sporting practices are historically produced, socially constructed, and culturally defined to serve the interests and needs of powerful groups in society was clearly missing.

Recognizing the Relevance of Feminism

Despite the growth of the sociology of sport in the 1970s, it was clear that girls and women were not represented in the studies and literature. By 1976 there were 13 texts and anthologies (all from the United States) with a sociology of sport focus. Of those, only three had a separate chapter or section devoted to females, and of some 200 separate articles in the anthologies, fewer than one tenth were written or cowritten by women. The material on females in these texts and anthologies represented less than 3 percent of the total content. This made me angry. Although I knew there was more research and scholarship about women than was being acknowledged, also I was becoming acutely aware of the male bias in sociology and that feminist sociologists were addressing this androcentric perspective, as were feminist scholars in the humanities and other social sciences.

There was little feminist scholarship to read in the late 1970s, but I searched out and consumed everything I could find with one objective in mind: applying it to the study of girls and women in sport. My published writing from this period, aside from attempting to expand the sociological knowledge base about females in sport, also represents a plea to my professional and academe colleagues in physical education and the sociology of sport to recognize the relevance of feminism.

I also needed to learn more about sociology, so I embarked on a self-directed reading course in the history of social thought, contemporary social theory, and the epistemological debates within social research methodology. I was helped in this by several colleagues, mostly male, who were engaged in producing radical critiques of sport in Western societies. They were reading social theorists like Anthony Giddens, Pierre Bourdieu, Paul Willis, Antonio Gramsci, and Raymond Williams and were attempting to apply theories of power, social reproduction and practice, and cultural struggle and production to an analysis of the historical and cultural construction of modern sport. I read their work as well as the theorists from whom they drew their inspiration. I also read with great fervour emerging feminist theory, which, for the most part, my colleagues and the social theorists ignored.

Slowly I came to two major insights. The first was that social psychological research, with its emphasis on sex roles and sex identity, not only demanded a substantive critique but was potentially harmful because it continued to perpetuate the very stereotypes we wished to eradicate. Within the context of women and sport research, social psychological research needed to be replaced by a gender and sport discourse that treated gender as a relational category just like class or race (see chapter 2). This led me to my second insight: For most radical theorists, class was *the* primary form of domination, and it was going to be a long, hard battle to get them to recognize the gender blindness of their critiques (see chapter 3).

By the mid-1980s I was no longer alone in recognizing the potential of feminist theory and analysis for gender relations and sport. Susan Birrell, herself one of those who has contributed significantly to the women in sport discourse, documented this work, although primarily in North America (Birrell, 1988). Certainly we all owe a debt to the earlier efforts of Eleanor Metheny, Marie Hart, Ellen Gerber, Jan Felshin, Pearl Berlin, Dorothy Harris, and Carole Oglesby. As Birrell suggests, the work of Hart and Felshin in particular should be singled out because it was ''grounded in a feminist sensibility, yet little theoretical work was available to help them frame their arguments'' (p. 468). A decade and more ago I was unduly critical of this work because in my view it lacked the necessary theoretical sophistication. In hindsight, now that I am in my 50s with a whole new generation of scholars coming up behind, my own work also lacks the sophistication I know they will bring. We are products of our times in ways we do not realize until we look back.

In the early days, my colleagues in sport and physical education—both male and female—were almost entirely resistant to feminism. Now, despite pockets of intransigence, there is a small but critical mass of feminist and pro-feminist scholars around the world whose focus is the sociological study of gender and sport. Their work appears regularly in the books, journals, and conference programs of our field.[5]

My nonsporting feminist colleagues are mostly bemused by my continuing fascination with sport. For them, the highly competitive, sometimes violent, overly commercialized sports world represents distinctly nonfeminist values and is a world they generally ignore. Few are active in sports, although some certainly exercise for health and well-being; for many, negative childhood experiences in school physical education turned them off long ago. In my women's studies classes, I have sometimes to overcome the initial negative reaction of a student who finds it difficult not to associate me with a much disliked PE teacher.

Despite this often schizophrenic existence, I have seen my task as advocating the inclusion of sport on the feminist agenda and ensuring that feminism is very much a part of the sport agenda. One way I have tried to do this is through my university's women's studies program, which I helped to establish. Over the years, I have taught and held a variety of administrative positions in the program. However, I still find it a struggle to get discussions about women's sport included in the women's studies curricula.

The remainder of this book traces my journey through various feminisms and my struggle to understand what they could contribute not only to our understanding of women in sport, but to our efforts to make the sports world a better place for women.

Notes

1. It is called "second-wave feminism" to distinguish it from the earlier women's rights movement, which came to a halt in many Western countries after the First World War when women were granted the right to vote. Dale Spender (1985), in *For the Record: The Making and Meaning of Feminist Knowledge*, reviews and interprets many of these classics, as well as others. It is well worth a read.

2. Paul Willis's conference paper was entitled "Performance and meaning: A socio-cultural view of women in sport" (September, 1973), but unfortunately there were no proceedings from the conference. A shortened version of his paper with the title "Women in sport [2]" was published in *Working Papers in Cultural Studies* 5 (Spring), 1974, 21-36. In that same volume there is a paper by C. Critcher ("Women in sport [1]"), which was also given at the Birmingham conference. For a version of my own contribution to this conference, see M.A. Hall (1976). Another

version of the Willis paper with the title "Women in sport in ideology" was published in Jennifer Hargreaves (Ed.), *Sport, Culture and Ideology* (pp. 117-35). London: Routledge & Kegan Paul, 1982. This version is also reprinted in S. Birrell & C.L. Cole (Eds.), *Women, Sport, and Culture* (pp. 31-45). Champaign, IL: Human Kinetics, 1994.

3. Title IX is a federal act that states: "No person in the United States shall, on the basis of sex, be excluded from participation in, be denied the benefits of, or be subjected to discrimination under any education program or activity receiving federal financial assistance." This legislation and its implementation significantly affected the growth of girls' high school and women's collegiate athletics.

4. A semantic differential is an instrument that measures meaning as a relational concept. A semantic scale is composed of a series of polar (opposite-in-meaning) adjectives: for example, happy-sad, fast-slow, aggressive-passive, hot-cold. Respondents are asked to rate or evaluate a particular concept, for example an "athletic woman," in relation to these polar adjectives. It is then possible to draw a profile, and obtain an overall score, of how respondents "rate" this particular concept.

5. We should, however, not become too complacent; there is still a sadly disproportionate amount of published work devoted to gender and/or feminism within the sociology of sport. For instance, of 15 authors and coauthors in Ingham and Loy (1993), a third are women; and out of 11 chapters only 2 are about gender or are explicitly feminist. In Dunning, Maguire, and Pearton (1993) only 1 of 13 authors/coauthors is a woman, and only 1 chapter of 12 is about women's sport despite the fact that the book purports to examine, among other factors, how sport development is affected by gender roles. See also Heinemann and Preuss (1990), Lock (1993), and Melnick and Sabo (1987) for useful content analyses of sociology of sport literature. Women and sport scholarship continues to be ghettoized—it remains outside the main(male)stream sociology of sport literature. Four recent examples, although as anthologies they are certainly useful in their own right, are Birrell and Cole (1994), Cohen (1993), Costa and Guthrie (1994), and Creedon (1994).

From Categoric to Relational Research

2

Several years ago I observed that it has been social psychology (to say nothing of biology and physiology), with its emphasis on the individual and individual differences to the exclusion of social and political factors, that has largely determined the discourse about gender and sport (M.A. Hall, 1988). How much has the discourse changed? In recent assessments of research on gender issues in sport (Dewar, 1993a) and on women of colour in sport (Y.R. Smith, 1992), three levels of analysis were identified: (a) *categoric research*, with a primary focus on quantifying and empirically studying sex or race differences in athletic participation, performance, and abilities, and attempting to explain their existence in terms of biological factors and socialization; (b) *distributive research*, which examines the distribution of resources (e.g., competitive opportunities, coaching positions, administrators, income levels, sponsorship) and focuses on inequality in opportunities, access, and financial resources; and (c) *relational analyses*, which begin with the assumption that sporting practices are historically produced, socially constructed, and culturally defined to serve the interests and needs of powerful groups in society. Sport, therefore, is seen as a cultural representation of social relations and here includes gender, class, and race relations.

All three of these forms of research are present today, but it is primarily developmental psychologists and social psychologists who conduct categoric research. It is called categoric because it focuses on the differences between categories—women and men, black and white, native and nonnative—and attempts to explain these differences through biology or socialization. A selection of topics within this framework would include female sport participation patterns (socialization, motivation), personality variables of female athletes, competition anxiety and performance, exercise behaviours, moral issues (aggression, rule-breaking, violence), and gender differences in sport involvement (cf. Lenskyj, 1991c, pp. 86-97; Lenskyj, 1994, pp. 7-15). In the case of women of colour, categoric research often focuses on the biology of the races and therefore cannot account for the complexities of social structures and power relations (Y.R. Smith, 1992). This approach concentrates on individuals, and what is usually missing is an analysis of the powerful ways in which gender and race relations are socially and historically produced.

Within the sociology of sport, distributive research on gender and race, or both together, is still very prominent. It is a valuable tool because it provides proof of unequal allocation of or unequal access to limited resources, and it can be used to plot progress, or the lack of it, over time. Nearly every aspect of inequality, whether in participation (club, school, university), competition (local, province/state, national, international), leadership (coaches, volunteers, administrators, officials), or media representation (coverage, portrayal, content/textual analyses), has been documented in many countries and sometimes over a long period. This kind of research produces useful knowledge about women's position, and it is sometimes used as a starting point for further analysis and action. However, as Y.R. Smith (1992) rightly points out, barriers to equality are not removed simply through a process of identification, nor are inequitable conditions unquestionably perceived as problematic; so, in the end, the power relations that constitute racism and sexism, or other ''isms,'' are rarely confronted.

Over the past few years, there have been an increasing number of calls for more theoretically informed relational analyses of gender, race, and ethnic issues in sport. Susan Birrell (1988, 1989, 1990) argues persuasively that gender and race relations are characterized by unequal relationships between dominant and subordinate groups, that sport plays a role in their construction and persistence, that they take specific forms in particular times, and that a critical analysis of the cultural and ideological practices determining these relations is essential. British sport sociologist Jennifer Hargreaves (1986, 1989, 1990, 1992, 1994) has consistently argued that we need to understand how, in sport as in other cultural activities, gender relations are part of a complex process specific to capitalist social relations. She advocates the use of hegemony theory[1] whereby history can be read as a series of struggles for power between dominant and subordinate groups. She also applies the concept of hegemony to male leadership and domination in leisure and sport in order "to show ways in which gender relations intersect with specific features of capitalist relations and patriarchal relations" (Jennifer Hargreaves, 1989, p. 134). In a review of the various approaches that have been used to explain male dominance and sex segregation in coaching, Annelies Knoppers (1992) asserts that researchers should no longer focus on the "qualifications of women (individual approach) or assume gender neutrality of structure, jobs, workers, or workplaces (structural approach)." What is needed instead is a social relational approach that shows how structures, jobs, activities in those jobs, workers, and places of work are gendered as women and men struggle collectively over the meaning of coaching. And finally, after reviewing the state of research about women of colour in sport, Yevonne Smith (1992) concluded, "It is important to begin more relational analyses of and by diverse women of colour and to understand how collective personal experiences and processes are informed by race, gender, and class power relations" (p. 224).

Certainly the discourse surrounding gender and sport has changed, and continues to change rapidly, as feminist theory and scholarship are used by more researchers and in a more sophisticated fashion than has previously been the case. Not everyone takes for granted gender as a relational concept, however, and much research can still be classified as either biological, categoric, or functionalist. In this chapter I discuss why this is still the case, point to the inadequacies of specific research within these broader categories, and show how feminist critiques have been invaluable to our understanding of these problems. I also review recent developments in the psychology of gender and sport, a field that is slowly becoming more attuned to a feminist critique.

Biologism: Tomboys and Gender Verification

Biologism is the preoccupation with biological explanations in the analysis of social situations. Since the 1970s there has been a resurgence of biological determinist theories explaining human behaviour and the structure of human societies. One recent sign is the increasing number of articles in popular magazines and television programs devoted to innate gender and race differences, the chemistry of aggressive behaviour, and the origins of homosexuality (e.g., the "gay" gene). Those who study these matters suggest that biologism made headway in the 1970s because neurobiologists began to unravel the genetic, hormonal, and neurodevelopmental processes involved in sexual differentiation (Byne & Parsons, 1993; Kaplan & Rogers, 1990; Rogers, 1988). In the 1980s it became unfashionable in some quarters to endorse either side of the nature/nurture debate because those who supported psychosocial explanations (including most feminists) were sufficiently influential in their critique of this simplistic dichotomy. What emerged was an uneasy truce, known as the *interactionist* approach, whereby biologic (hormonal and genetic) determinants were thought to exert at most a predisposing rather than determining influence as they interacted with psychosocial and environmental factors. Today the prominence of biological determinist theories is in reaction to the continuing influence of psychosocial or social constructionist explanations, and there is a propensity in the popular media to report "positive" findings when in fact there is no compelling evidence to support either a biologic theory or any singular psychosocial explanation.

Biological determinism forces thinking that is both reductionistic and categoric. Reductionism attempts to explain the properties of complex wholes in terms of the units that compose the whole: "For example, it is argued that the behaviour of a society can be explained on the basis of the individuals within it and, in turn, the behaviour of the latter can be explained in terms of the genetic constitution of each individual" (Rogers, 1988, p. 44). Therefore, in the case of sex differences, genes are said to play a causal role in determining male/female differences by being expressed through the sex hormones, which in turn act on the brain (referred to by some as "brain sex").

Reductionism also spawns thinking in terms of dichotomous categories: male versus female, male sex hormone versus female sex hormone, black versus white, and so forth. A dichotomy forces a polarization and ignores overlaps; differences are seen as more interesting than similarities, and there is a tendency to see these differences as absolute (Rogers, 1988). It is telling that within psychology there is a field of specialization called "sex differences" yet no equivalent "sex similarities."

All this is an introduction to my own excursions into these debates. In 1972 John Money and Anke Ehrhardt published *Man & Woman, Boy & Girl*, which sought to explain behaviour dimorphism (having two forms) and psychosexual differentiation in males and females. It was primarily through reading their work that I became fascinated by the potential influence of prenatal hormonal factors on individual psychosocial development. One statement in their book stood out above all the rest: "One may sum up the current findings by saying that genetic females masculinized in utero [in the womb] and reared as girls have *a high chance of being tomboys in their behavior*" (p. 10, my emphasis). Money and Ehrhardt's definition of tomboyism included a preference for vigorous athletic activity, especially outdoor pursuits. Added to this was the "fact" that genetic females could be subject to prenatal androgen excess without any virilizing effect on the external genitalia, although the excess might be sufficient to influence the brain during critical periods of development.

At one point in a class on women and sport I was discussing the evidence concerning the masculinizing effects of synthetic progestin with several athletically inclined females, who shortly thereafter contacted their mothers to ascertain if they had been treated with a synthetic steroid during pregnancy. None of them had, which made the students immediately suspicious of my theory; indeed, as it turns out, they should have been. It was a quantum leap to suggest that women who enjoy sports or who are skilled athletes have been prenatally "programmed" by some quirk of nature or a misused drug. I felt, nonetheless, that the whole matter had to be investigated further. What sort of evidence, I wondered, existed for a hormonal basis to sexually dimorphic behavior (i.e., having two forms, male and female), and particularly that behaviour characterized as athletic—outdoor, competitive, vigorous, and involving high energy expenditure?[2] For months I steeped myself in what was to me a very foreign literature, and, in the end, I concluded that there was simply no clear answer to my question.

I tell this story to illustrate just how important the feminist critiques of biology, sociobiology, and biological determinism in general have been to our understanding of human behaviour.[3] My quest to understand sexually dimorphic behavior was, as it turned out, both reductionist and categoric because biology itself provides no clear justification for a dichotomous view of gender. As many others have pointed out, it is impossible to classify accurately all humans into the restrictive categories of male and female because of the great variety of genetic types and hormonal conditions that characterize individuals (Shilling, 1993; see also Birke, 1992; Fausto-Sterling, 1993; and Kaplan & Rogers, 1990). Yet, the "simplistic once and for all either/or consignment of individuals to the categories of male/female" continues to influence questionable research that sometimes leads to equally questionable policy decisions (Shilling, 1993, p. 54). Let me illustrate the sort of biological determinism that still pervades our thinking about female athleticism with two examples: the case of tomboyism, and the pernicious gender verification of international competition.

When Money and Ehrhardt found a higher level of tomboyism in genetic females who had been subjected to prenatal androgen in excess of the exposure in normal controls, they interpreted the tomboyism as a masculinization of the developing brain. Their definition of tomboyism included a high level of physical energy expenditure, especially in vigorous outdoor play, games, and sport; a preference for male over female playmates; a preference for practical clothing and an indifference to personal adornments; a preference for toys traditionally reserved for boys; a lack of interest in dolls; little rehearsal of the traditional female role of wife and mother; a late interest in boyfriends and dating; and, eventually, the subordination of marriage to a career (Money & Ehrhardt, 1972, pp. 102-108).

Although feminists have pointed out flaws in the Money and Ehrhardt research (problems with the controls, the questionnaires used, the interviewing process, the sexist language, and the underlying assumptions),[4] their studies have been widely and uncritically cited in the scientific and popular literatures. Bad science aside, the fact that tomboyism is entirely a cultural phenomenon is also ignored. In fact, the term "tomboy" illustrates perfectly our belief in a sex-dichotomized world.[5] Over time, "tom" came to be used as a generic term for anything male; in fact, the very early (i.e., 16th century) usage of tomboy referred to a boy—particularly a rude, boisterous, or impudent one—who acted too much like a tom, or a man. Before long, the term was also used to describe "bold, wild, or immodest" women (in some parts of Britain, for example, prostitutes are still called "toms" or "tommys"). Eventually, tomboy came to mean a spirited young girl who "behaves like a boisterous boy." Why do we not refer to boys as "marygirls" when they display sissy behavior? (There is no need, since they are simply called "girls" or, more often, derogatory sexual terms for females.)

Quite simply, scientists who use tomboyism as a measure of sexually dimorphic behaviour and who refuse to acknowledge its cultural history are engaging in circular reasoning:

> In the act of naming the disease "tomboyism," they already impute to it a cause—namely, a woman imitating a man's behavior. They then name the possessors of the disease "fetally *masculinized* genetic females," thus doubly reinforcing the cause—of course, the "tomboy" is a "masculinized" female. Finally, they formally name the cause "a *masculinizing* effect on the fetal brain." Proof is executed: A equals A equals A. (Fried, 1982, p. 60)

One hears the word tomboy less and less today, at least in everyday parlance, because in our less sex-dichotomized society most young girls are involved in some form of organized sport, wear jeans everywhere, spurn frilly clothes, and, through the example of their mothers, see the possibility (and the problems) of combining work and family. Yet, social scientists and especially psychologists still seem determined to perpetuate the myth. As I wrote this, I noticed in the newspaper that researchers at Northwestern University were looking for tomboys between the ages of four and nine who will be studied alongside a control group of sissy siblings who prefer activities traditionally regarded as feminine.

Related to tomboyism as a sex-dichotomized concept is the highly controversial "gender verification" testing in competitive sport whereby women who wish to compete *as women* must prove that they are really women and not men cheating. Since its introduction in 1966, "femininity control" as it used to be called, has been criticized by the medical and scientific communities because it does not achieve its aim of excluding men from women's competitions. It has in fact wrongly eliminated some women athletes with genetic disorders that confer no physical advantage. The test used, sex chromatin analysis, was long ago abandoned by the genetic community because erroneous interpretations, yielding both false negative and false positive results, are not uncommon in inexperienced hands.[6]

Except for the International Amateur Athletic Federation, which in 1992 decided to abolish gender verification, testing is still required by most international sport federations, including the International Olympic Committee. The world of sport, like most of society, is premised on the assumption that there are two sexes—male and female—and that it is always possible to prove that you are one or the other. If you are not one, then you must be the other, or you are masquerading as such.

Today, however, we know much more about "intersexuality," which means that the sex of a person's upbringing does not match one or more of their biological sex characteristics (for example, chromosomal constitution, or having ovaries or testes).[7] Biological sex, as respected medical scientist Anne Fausto-Sterling (1993) points out, is a vast, infinitely malleable continuum that defies categorization. In addition, members of the "transgender" community (preoperative, postoperative, and nonsurgical transsexuals, as well as male and female cross-dressers and transvestites) are becoming increasingly vocal about the possibilities of numerous genders and multiple social identities (Bolin, 1994).[8]

Gender verification in sport has come under scrutiny because it says nothing about the sex of an individual from an anatomical, physiological, and psychosocial standpoint. This criticism led a working group within the International Amateur Athletic Federation to propose that individuals who are legally, socially, and psychologically females from childhood be eligible to compete in women's events irrespective of their genetic, chromosomal, gonadal, and hormonal sex (Ljungqvist & Simpson, 1992). It was also recommended that individuals undergoing sex reassignment from male to female before puberty should be regarded as girls and women. In the case of transsexuals (male to female) reassigned after puberty, the federation proposed that decisions concerning eligibility be made by the relevant medical body within the sport organization concerned. As for gender verification itself, the IAAF decided that a medical examination for the health and well-being of *all* athletes participating in international competitions would suffice since it would include a simple inspection of the external genitalia. Moreover, given that routine drug testing requires the voiding of urine to be carefully observed by an official, the likelihood of a man masquerading as a woman is extremely remote. These are sound decisions, and we can only hope that eventually all sport organizations, including the International Olympic Committee, will abolish gender testing.

The preceding examples of tomboyism and gender verification illustrate the pitfalls of biologism, and, in particular, biological reductionism. For a girl, behaving like a boy is culturally relative, and using what amounts to questionable scientific evidence to claim a biological basis for tomboyism is not only bad science, but it is tautological reasoning. I would also argue that psychological research into what "causes" tomboyism is misguided and totally unnecessary. Gender verification is an example of the interests of sport (as is true of the state) in maintaining a two-sex system, which, as we have seen, is in defiance of nature. In their misguided efforts to protect female competitors from men masquerading as women, the International Olympic Committee and other controlling bodies perpetuate the myth that our sex is determined by our chromosomes alone.

In sum, biologism is insupportable because, as Shilling (1993) argues, "The structure of society is explained not only on the basis of the individuals within it, but the intentions, actions and potential of individuals are explained as a result of some aspect of their physical or genetic constitution" (p. 68). This sort of reductionistic thinking leads to dichotomous categorization whereby individuals are divided into simplistic social categories, like male/female and black/white, which stress differences and ignore similarities and overlaps. These social categories are then reified as natural phenomenon when, in fact, they are *simultaneously* social and biological: "They hover between the earth of biology and the heaven of history, resident in neither because citizens of both; and the pressure from each realm irons out the wrinkles proper to the other" (Connell, 1983, p. 57).

In terms of gender, the sports world has by and large treated these categories as biological entities by creating the binary of "men's sport" and "women's sport." It is important to point out that for the most part both men *and* women have wanted it that way. In a provocative essay, sport sociologist Mary Jo Kane (1995) observes that we rarely acknowledge (or analyze) sport as a "continuum" whereby *people* of varying height, weight, size, strength, age, and ability play sport, and that the division of sport into gender categories has historically been for social, not biological reasons. Sport sociologists have focused primarily on the ways in which modern sport is used to construct and promote an ideology of "natural" gender difference and the inferiority of women. But at the same time, Kane argues, we have created beliefs in and practices about the binary while simultaneously suppressing evidence of the continuum. The debates over separation and integration in women's sport have a long history, and they are taken up again in the last chapter.

Culture, Femininity, and Athleticism

From the 1960s onward a major focus of gender issues within North American sport sociology and social psychology was to "prove" that sport competition did not masculinize female participants either psychologically or behaviourally. The literature followed, to a certain extent, the major trends in the larger sex role/sex identity research of psychology. The earlier research was concerned primarily with the perceptions, stereotypes, and acceptance of the female athlete. Much of this work coincided with increasing numbers of female physical educators entering Canadian and American graduate programs whose personal concerns about the myths surrounding athleticism and femininity were reflected in the thesis topics they chose.

Within the social sciences, particularly psychology, there was a long history of assuming that so-called cross-sex behaviours and preferences (e.g., athleticism among females) were indicators of emotional disturbance or sexual deviation. To be a woman and an athlete was to be in conflict and therefore psychologically unhealthy. With the reemergence of feminism in the 1960s and the remarkable explosion of feminist scholarship in the succeeding three decades, these assumptions have been not only challenged but investigated with increasing rigor, sophistication, and tenacity.

The key construct to emerge was psychological androgyny, the premise of which was that masculinity and femininity are independent rather than bipolar dimensions, so that individuals high on both (called androgynes) are mentally healthier and socially more effective. Sport researchers leapt upon this concept, and their studies typically found that female athletes were more androgynous, more masculine, less sex-typed, or less feminine than female nonathletes but were no less psychologically healthy and often had a more positive self-concept.

In a substantive critique of this research (M.A. Hall, 1981), I argued that since androgyny simply combines the old dualities of masculinity and femininity, which are themselves socially constructed, the concept and the working models that define it will do little to bring about real change in a society that is fundamentally oppressive to women. This of course was a political view and one that I still hold. Later (M.A. Hall, 1988) I pointed out that the important sociological question is not whether a conflict between gender and culture exists, but why it exists only in the realm of the feminine.

As Rosenblum (1986) so cogently argues, a key feature in the American conception of gender (and in other Western cultures as well) is the care/autonomy distinction: Femininity is equated with and displayed by care for others rather than self, whereas masculinity is characterized by autonomy, self-reliance, and achievement requiring an asocial, or even antisocial, stance to the world. Prevailing values, however, stress achievement, individuality, and self-promotion. Femininity must forego these values to be true to a feminine morality with its emphasis on self-sacrifice and responsiveness to others' needs. For example, research in a variety of countries has shown how women "service" men's and children's leisure and lack any sense of "entitlement" to enjoy their own leisure. Men, on the other hand, dominate local recreational resources and activities, and often deliberately exclude women.[9]

Therefore, the conflict between gender and culture exists only in the realm of the feminine because cultural practices, like sport and leisure, are defined by masculine standards. To me this explained the almost obsessive need by American sport researchers in particular to explore the conflict relationship between femininity (never masculinity) and sport and to "prove" that female athletic involvement had positive psychological benefits without producing a loss of femininity.[10] I also suggested, as did others, that in reality femininity was a thinly disguised code word for heterosexuality. The real issue behind so much attention to an athlete's femininity was the fear that she might be a lesbian.

Statements like the following, which are from only two of the myriad of studies along these lines, illustrate how normal, self-fulfilling activities like participation in sports for girls or in dance for boys are considered sex-typed or cross-sex-typed (even deviant) in a psychological sense:

> The results of this investigation show that female athletes apparently do not experience much role conflict, can be more M without being less F, and tend to have higher levels of self-concept—particularly in areas most logically related to sporting experience. The findings strongly refute the popular myth that female athletes are not, and cannot be, feminine. (Jackson & Marsh, 1986, p. 208)

> One possible explanation concerns the relationship between engaging in gender-deviant activities and the culturally established value of the activities. Let us assume, for the purposes of argument, that masculine activities are indeed perceived as more valuable than feminine activities in our culture. For the cross-sex-typed woman, cross-gender identification may make gender-deviant behavior (participation in masculine activities) more likely. (Matteo, 1986, p. 430)

What is frustrating is that this sort of research continues to be published in respectable psychology journals. Between 1965 and 1987, when I last did an assessment, I had amassed over 70 published articles, conference papers, and theses of this type. Although I no longer collect these studies, I certainly notice them in the literature: "Social Acceptability of Sport for Young Women" (Germone & Furst, 1991); "Perceived Effects on Femininity of the Participation of Women in Sport" (Pedersen & Kono, 1990); "Sex-Role Conflict in Female Athletes: A Possible Marker for Alcoholism" (Wetzig, 1990); and "Gender-Role Orientations of Male and Female Coaches of a Masculine-Typed Sport" (Wrisberg, 1990). In their conclusions, the authors of these highly simplistic studies often express surprise that female athletes possess socially desirable characteristics/behaviours and that sport participation does not detract from their femininity. Even in more sophisticated studies utilizing up-to-date psychological theories (for example, gender schema theory, which suggests that individuals with a propensity for sex-typing are more likely than cross-sex-typed individuals to classify sports in gender terms), there is still the unavoidable reification whereby behaviours become real when in fact they are abstract concepts:

> The results for cross-sex typed individuals were very similar to those of sex-typed individuals, suggesting the gender schematicity of both groups. Both groups gave gender-based reasons for rejecting sex-inappropriate sports, rated gender-based reasons as important to their decisions, and formed masculine impressions of others thought to enjoy masculine sports and feminine impressions of others thought to enjoy feminine sports. Partial support was also obtained for the

prediction that cross-sex-typed males and females would display somewhat different patterns of behavior. Males' reasons for rejecting sex-inappropriate sports were significantly more gender stereotyped than females' reasons. Thus, the cross-sex-typed person appears as gender schematic as the sex-typed person. (Matteo, 1988, p. 55)

Aside from my doubt that this sort of research can help individuals become less or more sex-typed, cross-sex-typed, or whatever, it has hindered political attempts to critique and change the pervasive gender ideologies of our culture. Ellen Gerber (1973), a physical educator (now lawyer) who made a significant contribution to the field in the early 1970s, observed that the construct "sex-role identity" was premised on an erroneous and inherently destructive assumption. In order to have a sex-role identification, she argued, there must be two separate sex roles, an idea she found unpalatable. "Even to study these ideas," she argued, "is to help to perpetuate them" (p. 8). Unfortunately in the 20 years since, a veritable psychological industry has been established to study precisely these constructs.

The Inadequacy of Role Theory and Functionalism

The term *sex role* (or gender role) is now so common that many new researchers coming into the field do not realize there is a very substantive critique both of the notion of sex role and role in general.

In my original 1981 critique, I outlined the following major concerns about the sex roles notion: (a) It is sociologically illogical in that we do not speak of race roles (or age roles or class roles) because we do not attempt to explain differential behavior patterns on the basis of race, age, or social class alone, but we do explain them in terms of a power differential that certainly coincides with race, class, and age distinctions; (b) the notion of role focuses attention more on individuals than on social structure and depoliticizes the central questions of power and control in explaining gender inequality; (c) terms like "sex role stereotyping," "sex role socialization," and "sex role orientation" are used as if they exist concretely rather than being analytical constructs, in other words, they become reified; and (d) role terminology is not fully applicable to gender because sex or gender, like age, race, and social class, infuse the more specific social roles one plays (e.g., teacher, athlete, coach, university professor).

Carolyn Sherif (1982), a social psychologist whose work was well-known in the 1960s and 1970s (until her early death in 1982), likened the term "sex roles" to a "boxcar carrying an assortment of sociological and psychological data along with an explosive mixture of myth and untested assumptions" (p. 392). More significantly she argued that stereotypical attributions of instrumental versus expressive behaviour, which are the ısis of sex roles and are seen as universal, are part of the very ideology that inhibit women's entry into more egalitarian role relationships with men. Her advice, never taken by the discipline of psychology, was to drop the concept altogether.

Several sociologists (e.g., Connell, 1983; Coulson, 1972; Giddens, 1979), although more concerned with the general concept of role than with the more specific sex role, have also proposed that the concept be abandoned, certainly by sociologists. Anthony Giddens pointed out that within functionalist theories of social systems, role (to quote Talcott Parsons) is "the primary point of direct articulation between the personality of the individual and the structure of the social system." In order for society to "function," it was theorized, there needs to be reciprocity between people based on their various roles. For Giddens, and others (including myself) who eschew functionalism, "Social systems are not constituted of roles but of (reproduced) practices; and it is practices, not roles which (via the duality of structure) have to be regarded as the 'points of articulation' between actors and structures" (p. 117).

This is an important point because the concept of sex (or gender) roles is a functionalist conception of gender deeply shaped by the concepts—instrumental versus expressive—developed by Parsons and used by others (Stacey & Thorne, 1985). The implication is that gender is thought to be more central to the family than to other institutions (sport is a good example here) and that gender arrangements function primarily to ensure social maintenance and reproduction. What is interesting is that functionalist assumptions are more deeply ingrained in sociological conceptions of gender than in other forms of social inequality like class or race.

Since, as I pointed out in the first chapter, much of the early women and sport research was within a psychological or social psychological perspective, it was inevitable that gender role "deviance" (girls and women taking up sport) needed an explanation. One way to interpret their involvement (or lack of it) is through "socialization" and more specifically "gender role socialization." Therefore, within the social learning framework, girls and boys are differentially influenced by socializing "agents" (siblings, peers, teachers, coaches, role models) and socializing "situations" (family, school, and other environments), and as a result end up being differentially involved in sport (Greendorfer, 1992, 1993). Girls who persist in opposing pressure not to take up sport (tomboys for example) are explained via "imperfect" socialization, or better still, by overcoming "role conflict" between their role as a girl/woman and their role as an athlete. One problem with the role conflict theory is that it does not hold up well when tested empirically. Study after study shows that female athletes perceive and experience little or no role conflict (Allison, 1991). Both explanations, as Connell (1983) suggests, ignore the element of resistance, in this case among young women, to social pressure and control.

Functionalist conceptions of gender applied to sport have failed to theorize femininity (and masculinity) as socially constructed, historically specific, and mediated by social class, race, ethnicity, and other social categories. From a practical perspective, we learn little about how specific socialization practices serve the interests of dominant groups in our society by making their privileges seem either natural or deserved. It is important to connect the analysis of social inequality and the power structures of society with the meanings and values associated with participation in sport. Socialization is more than just a routine or natural process whereby individuals learn skills, traits, values, attitudes, norms, and knowledge associated with a particular social or gender role (M.A. Hall, Slack, Smith, & Whitson, 1991). As I suggest in the next chapter, it would be much more productive to examine the historical roots and precursors of women's struggle to enter the sports world with a view to explaining ongoing and contemporary issues.

Sport Psychology: The Need for a Politicized Feminism

The conceptualization of gender and the subsequent research focus taken today by sport psychologists and sport sociologists is now considerably different. It would be wrong to conclude that all sport psychologists interested in gender conduct only categoric research, that is research with a specific focus on sex differences. Diane Gill (1992, 1994a, 1994b), in comprehensive reviews of existing research on the role of gender in sport and exercise behaviour, shows how there has been a shift away from an emphasis on biologically based sex differences and psychosocially based gender differences to more social cognitive constructs and models (e.g., achievement cognitions, gender belief systems). She argues that sport psychologists should adopt a "true *social*-psychological perspective," meaning that research must be placed in a broader sociohistorical and cultural context. Gill does not advocate that sport psychologists become sociologists to study gender, rather she claims that "sound sport psychology research on gender beliefs and processes within the social context of sport and exercise could advance our overall understanding of gender and sport" (1992, p. 156). She also advocates three basic steps for achieving a feminist approach to sport psychology: recognize that gender does make a difference, incorporate feminist scholarship about gender, and translate gender scholarship into feminist sport psychology *practice* (1994b). I will return to the notion of feminist practice momentarily, but first I want to make a few observations.

Diane Gill is at the forefront among sport psychologists calling for a feminist perspective within the field. Certainly others (e.g., Dewar & Horn, 1992; Duquin, 1994a; Fasting, 1993; Krane, 1994) have critiqued traditional research methods and epistemological positions, challenging sport psychologists to develop and use alternative frameworks, including a feminist paradigm. However, what I find interesting is that none of these critics has paid much attention to the evolving debates among feminist psychologists and social psychologists about the implications of the inter-section between psychology and feminism. It is difficult to summarize the current state of these discussions, and readers should examine the sources for themselves because I cannot do justice here to the depth and sophistica-tion of this material.[11]

Nonetheless, a good place to begin is to recognize that psychology as a discipline has alternated between two basic paradigms that explain the relationship between humans and their environment: Reality constructs the person versus the person constructs reality (Unger, 1989). In the first paradigm reality is stable, irreversible, and deterministic; it is discoverable through the proper application of scientific methodology; and individual differences are a result of the impingement of that reality on the developing organism. Behaviourism, psychoanalysis, and sociobiology, although diverse schools of thought, represent this paradigm best because they do not question the existence of a reality "out there." In the second (person constructs reality) paradigm, reality is largely a matter of historical and cultural definition and the individual has an active role in constructing his or her own reality. Psychologists who take this viewpoint see themselves as "social construc-tionists."

It is the social constructionist paradigm that has appealed to feminist psychologists rather than either behaviourism or sociobiology, although there are feminist derivatives of classic psychoanalytic theory (for example, the "French feminism" of Luce Irigary and Hélène Cixous). It is within the social constructionist paradigm that the new psychology of sex and gender has become established, and there is now a substantial body of research on sex-related differences in social behaviours. This research has led to cognitive theories about sex and gender (e.g., gender role orientation, gender and achievement orientations, gender schema theory, gender belief systems). As has already been mentioned, some sport psychologists have tapped into this new knowledge and applied it to their own research (see Gill, 1992, 1994a, for a review).

There are those, however, who are critical of feminist psychology for its focus on between-gender differences. Michelle Fine and Susan Gordon (1989) make three important arguments about the gender difference formu-lation. These arguments are: (a) it creates, as it legitimates, a powerful and unarticulated commitment to heterosexuality as the frame for social research on gender (p. 152); (b) it obscures the political and/or psychoana-lytic insight that to be male or masculine in our culture is *not* to be female or feminine, and it reproduces the false splitting of the masculine from the feminine (p. 153); and (c) it renders the study of differences among and intimacy between women as either irrelevant to social theory or plainly bad science (p. 153).

Mainstream psychologists, argue Fine and Gordon (1989), disparge the study of women alone—without a comparison group of men—as inadequate research despite the fact that many psychological "facts" are based on studies of men alone. In sum, they charge that psychology has

appropriated and depoliticized feminism in two ways: through the search for gender differences and through the presumption of gender neutrality. The argument for *neutrality* suggests that no feminist effort need be asserted to unpack power, context, or meaning; and the search for gender *differences* flattens the asymmetries that organize gender relations while promoting heterosexuality as the exclusive frame for viewing social relations. (p. 157)

These critics and others are arguing for a *political* feminist psychology. Otherwise feminists can fit all too easily into psychology by pretending it is an apolitical discipline; by representing themselves uncritically as "objective" researchers; by conducting gender-neutral analyses without discussing power, social context, and meanings; and by "constructing the rich and contradictory consciousness of girls and women into narrow factors and scales" (Fine & Gordon, 1989, p.168). To focus on power, however, is to treat gender as a relational category rather than as a characteristic of individuals. Psychology has traditionally focused on the individual and the personal, and to do otherwise would be to cross over into sociology or political science (Kitzinger, 1991). There are certainly voices within feminist psychology calling for a more creative, subversive, theoretically incisive, and radical approach, but whether or not mainstream/malestream psychology will ever be transformed by feminist scholarship remains to be seen.

As discussed earlier, some sport psychologists have begun to think about the issues raised by feminist psychologists, which are primarily a matter of epistemology, not methodology, and to examine the implications for a reconstituted psychology of sport. Perhaps the most useful of this work extends these theoretical discussions to sport psychology *practice*, and again, sport psychologist Diane Gill has led the way. In a recent discussion (Gill, 1994b), which borrows heavily from the feminist therapy literature, she focuses primarily on sport psychology practice and consultation within the educational context. She considers how sport psychologists can (and should) translate gender scholarship into feminist practice. Her suggestions include: Avoid sexist assumptions, standards, and practices; investigate variations of feminist therapy; emphasize neglected women's experiences (e.g., sexual harassment and homophobia); and "take a more nonhierarchical, empowering, process-oriented approach that shifts emphasis from personal change to social change" (p. 419). It has been a long time coming, but feminist scholarship is bringing women's experiences from their marginalized status in sport psychology to the centre and is recognizing that the guiding principles of feminist practice are applicable to both genders.

Notes

1. The notion of "hegemony" was developed in the 1930s by Italian political theorist Antonio Gramsci. Privileged groups in society are able— seemingly by consent—to establish their own cultural practices as the most valued and legitimate, whereas subordinate groups (e.g., blacks, natives, women) must struggle and fight against having their alternative practices and activities incorporated into the dominant sporting culture. Important to hegemony are resistance and struggle; it is an ongoing process because alternative cultural forms and practices always pose a threat to dominant ones. For more information, see M.A. Hall, Slack, Smith, & Whitson, 1991, especially chapters 2 and 3.

2. Fortunately, I never did publish my "quantum leap," although there is a conference paper on the topic (M.A. Hall, 1977). A more reasoned discussion appears later in M.A. Hall (1984a), some of which I have used in this section.

3. See, for example, Birke (1986), Bleier (1984), Fausto-Sterling (1992), Hubbard, Henifin, and Fried (1982), and Sayers (1982). See also Shilling (1993), especially his chapter on the "naturalistic body," because it provides a useful summary of this literature.

4. See in particular Bleier (1984, pp. 97-101), Fausto-Sterling (1992, pp. 133-141), and Fried (1982).

5. As I was writing this section, an informative little article on the origin of the word "tomboy" appeared in the Canadian national paper (see Cochrane, 1995). I am grateful to its author for this information.

6. The literature on this topic is now quite extensive: See, for example, Carlson (1991), de la Chapelle (1986), Fastiff (1992), Ferguson-Smith and Ferris (1991), Ferris (1992), Hipkin (1993), and Ljungqvist and Simpson (1992).

7. The standard medical literature, according to Fausto-Sterling (1993), uses the term "intersex" as a catch-all for three major subgroups with some mixture of male and female characteristics: true hermaphrodites who possess one testis and one ovary, the male pseudohermaphrodites who have testes and some aspects of the female genitalia but no ovaries, and the female pseudohermaphrodites who have ovaries and some aspects of the male genitalia but lack testes. However, the percentage of male and female characteristics can vary enormously among members of the same subgroup.

8. On this point, see Bornstein (1994), Herdt (1994), and Rothblatt (1995). In her book, Martine Rothblatt argues that "in a world free from the apartheid of sex, there would be no sex testing because there would be no sex-segregated athletic competition" (p. 73).

9. See, for example, Dempsey (1989) in Australia; Green, Hebron, and Woodward (1987) in England; Henderson and Dialeschki (1991) in the

United States; Hunter and Whitson (1991) in Canada; and Thompson (1992) in Australia.

10. There is now a welcome and growing body of research and scholarship around the topic of ''masculinity and sport'' (see chapter 3).

11. The collections I have found most helpful are Bohan (1992), Crawford and Gentry (1989), Fine (1992), Wilkinson (1986), and the British journal *Feminism & Psychology*, which began in 1991 (see especially articles in the first issue).

The Potential
of Feminist Cultural
Studies

3 In this chapter I examine the meaning, potential, and implications of feminist cultural studies applied to sport.[1] Central to the discussion is my belief that sociology, and by implication the sociology of sport and leisure, must be politically engaged and that there can be no dichotomy between one's role as a citizen and as a scientist. One of the most important insights of feminism is that our theory, politics, and practice are inextricably linked such that those working in academe, whose focus is research and scholarship, must work with those on the front line—be they participants, competitors, teachers, coaches, professional and volunteer leaders, policy-makers, or activists—so that together we are doing critical political work to bring about change. I begin here with a discussion of the sort of theory I think we need, and in subsequent chapters I examine the relationship between our research, as feminists, and our political practices. My placement of theory in one chapter and activism in another should not be construed as contradictory to what I have just said. I firmly believe in *praxis*, the notion that there should be unity between theory and action.

The Need for Theory

What theory or theories best suit our needs? Perhaps a more basic question is, why do we need theory anyway? One of the best discussions of these questions comes from Nancy Fraser, an American feminist philosopher engaged for some time in a critical analysis of feminism and social theory (see especially Fraser, 1989). She suggests that there are at least four reasons why feminists would want and need theory. First, it can help us understand how people's social realities are fashioned and altered over time. One must, Fraser (1992) argues, "study the historically specific social practices through which cultural descriptions of gender are produced and circulated" (p. 52). Later in this chapter, I stress the importance of an historical understanding of the gendering of sport, and, in particular, women's struggle to negotiate their contested place in the sports world. Social identities are also complex and plural, which is why we must pay much more attention to diversity among women based on differences in class, race, ethnicity, and sexual orientation as we reconstruct the historical record.

Second, Fraser states, theory can help us understand how, under conditions of inequality, people come together, form collective identities, and constitute themselves as collective social agents. Again, we need to reconstruct the struggles of women in sport, both among ourselves and against others, as we have tried either to resist the dominant sporting culture by providing separate alternatives for girls and women or to incorporate ourselves and women's sport into the structures of power. Closely connected is Fraser's third reason for the need for theory, which is to understand how the cultural hegemony of dominant groups in society is secured and contested. There is now a substantial body of theoretically nuanced scholarship on, for example, the ways in which sport is used to construct and promote an ideology of natural difference and inferiority, how these ideologies are embedded in media representations of gender, how bodies are gendered through various sporting practices, and how the relationship between sport and masculinity is increasingly problematic.

Lastly, theory should shed some light on the prospects for emancipatory social change and political practice. In Fraser's (1992) words, "The sort of theory I have been proposing would help us to understand how, even under conditions of subordination, women participate in the making of culture" (p. 54). Theory will not be able to tell us what to do in specific circumstances, but it should help us to understand our culture much better than we do now, pick apart how it works, and unravel the various interconnections that keep it together. In the end, theory raises our consciousness level and helps us to provide an ongoing critique of our culture, in this case, our sporting culture.

The question now becomes *what* theory can best help us understand identities, groups, hegemony, and emancipatory practice? The first point to reiterate is that unless theory is rooted in practice, it becomes prescriptive, exclusive, and elitist (Christian, 1987). American writer, teacher, and intellectual bell hooks (1994) puts it this way: "When our lived experience of theorizing is fundamentally linked to processes of self-recovery, of collective liberation, no gap exists between theory and practice" (p. 61). The second point is about the style of our discourse. If those of us who are committed to a more theoretically informed feminist politics of sport want to bring others who are less certain about the value of the project on board, then our theorizing must be relevant to sport and developed in clear, precise, accessible language. If it is not, then only the theorists will read and understand the theory, which seems so far removed from the everyday struggles of women on the "battlefield" of sport. It is vitally important for those women to understand (and read) what is being said by feminist scholars and theorists.

Today we are in a new theoretical era, one different from the past when theoretical concepts like gender stereotyping, role conflict, socialization, and role models and mentors made sense (see chapter 2). Now we need to focus on sport as a site for relations of domination and subordination (gender, race, class, sexuality, and other forms) *and* on how sport serves as a site of resistance and transformation.

The general consensus among those calling for relational analyses of gender and sport is for a feminist critique within the cultural studies tradition, or, more specifically, feminist cultural studies applied to sport. What is reflected here are two major movements within the broader framework known as the "radical" critiques of modern sport. One is the claim by feminists writing about sport that these critiques rely exclusively on mainstream (more accurately *male*stream) theorists, foreground class relations at the expense of other power relations, and take little or no account of feminist theorizing and scholarship. The second movement, dating from the late 1970s, reflects the rapidly shifting intellectual ground under feminism. Today we are besieged by a dizzying array of theoretical positions within feminist discourse and politics, including cultural hegemony, materialism, discourse theory, revisionary psychoanalysis, theories of representation, and, of course, poststructuralism and postmodernism. Most feminists writing about the social and cultural significance of sport and leisure are likely immersed in, and probably confused by, these shifting debates. The discourse, therefore, about gender and sport has changed significantly and continues to evolve.

Radical Critiques of Sport: Still Gender-Blind?

It is now more readily accepted that the significance of sport[2] in modern/postmodern life can only be grasped through an analysis of culture. Sport is such a visible aspect of popular culture, at least in the so-called developed countries where the cultural meanings and values enacted through participation, competition, and spectacle help make and remake us both as individuals and as collectivities. Sport, like other cultural forms and practices that become institutionalized, is profoundly affected by (and in turn affects) existing structures of power and inequality in those societies. With the recent publication of several "critical" textbooks in the sociology of sport, students increasingly are being asked to think critically about sport in their respective societies.[3] The difference between these texts and more traditional ones is that sociology is treated as a historical and critical science whereby it is important to bring a "sociological imagination" to the study of sport and to demonstrate the significance of a central problem of sociology: the explanation of structures of gender, class, racial, and ethnic inequalities. These recent textbooks are not gender-blind because they focus on the structures of organized sport that reflect and reinforce established patterns of gender inequality, as well as those of class, race, and ethnicity. Simplistic chapters on women in sport have been replaced by more sophisticated and nuanced discussions of social inequality and conflict, including inequality and conflict based on gender.

While these texts show promise, the picture is not as encouraging on the theoretical front. Although critiques of sport as a positive force in modernity emerged sporadically in the first half of the 20th century, the elaboration and extension of these ideas did not occur until the late 1960s and early 1970s with the advent of the "countercultural" criticism of sport posed by such writers as Jean-Marie Brohm in France (*Critiques du sport*), Bero Rigauer (*Sport und arbeit*) and Gerhard Vinnai (*Fußballsport als ideologie*) in Germany, and Paul Hoch (*Rip Off the Big Game*) in the United States (Gruneau, 1993). These writers, and others, were critical of consumer culture, the politics of spectacle, and the politics of the body, anticipating, as Gruneau points out, the present-day critiques of modernism and the subsequent debates over the existence of the postmodern condition. The earlier critiques, however, with their reliance on classical Marxism, could not accommodate the realities of modern oppression, including racial and sexual oppression, technocratic rationality, bureaucratic domination, and scientism, all of which existed independent of class and capital. The conclusion of the early radical critics of sport was that modern sport, like modern societies, was inherently totalitarian, leaving no way, intellectually at least, to explore the popularity and positive characteristics of modern sports as well as their oppositional and emancipatory possibilities.

Throughout the 1970s and 1980s, critical work on sport in Western societies struggled to free itself from this earlier heritage, namely what Gruneau calls radical pessimism and romantic antimodernism. For him (see Gruneau, 1983), and others such as John Hargreaves (1986) in Britain, it was necessary to develop a more adequate understanding of human agency and to construct a new theory of power, social practice, and cultural struggle. Gruneau turned for inspiration to the work of Anthony Giddens on structuration, Pierre Bourdieu on practices and rules, Paul Willis on social reproduction, Antonio Gramsci on hegemony, and Raymond Williams on language, ideology, and cultural production. Gruneau's study is a skillful analysis of how privileged groups in 19th-century Canadian society were able—seemingly by consent—to establish their own cultural practices as the most valued and legitimate, whereas subordinate groups (natives, underclasses, minorities) fought against having their alternative practices and activities incorporated into the dominant sporting culture.

Moving Beyond Class

An instructive debate took place in the *Sociology of Sport Journal* initiated by Rosemary Deem (1988) who argued that newer traditions in British sociology of sport (Weberian/figurational, neo-Marxist, and cultural studies) were still dominated by the view that class was the most important struggle and that gender was something women worry about.[4] Those who were willing to take gender (or race, age, or ethnicity) into account did so only if it could be accommodated without shifting the focus and debate too far from class. Feminist analyses of sport and leisure, on the other hand, failed to incorporate other issues like class, race, the state, ethnicity, and consumerism. Deem argued for the development of alliances among the different perspectives and the use of a more radical pluralist approach that does not assume *a priori* the superiority of one domination over another.

Responding to Deem, Robert Sparks (1988) noted that the complexity of such an undertaking should not be underestimated and suggested Gramsci's theory of hegemony[5] as a "tidy package" that allowed for empirical analyses as well as critical intervention. Deem (1989) countered by suggesting that we must look to a variety of perspectives because it is fundamental to the feminist theoretical project to develop a form of analysis that does not marginalize either gender or race over class *and* is tied solidly to political practice. David Whitson (1989), responding to both Deem and Sparks, supported the latter's contention that hegemony offered some useful possibilities for collaboration and acknowledged Deem's point that there is little critical scholarship by men that is informed by feminist writing, and even less in the sociology of sport.

Although this debate took place several years ago, I have seen little in the interim that suggests the situation is different today.[6] In fact, Charles Critcher (1986) said it all much earlier: "The principled and theoretical point is that we cannot and must not produce a supposedly radical theory of sport that is as gender-blind (in some cases more so) as the conventional wisdom we seek to supplant" (p. 338). Nor should we employ theoretical frameworks that privilege gender oppression over other forms of oppression. In a more recent discussion, Michael Messner (1990b) argues that studies of masculinity and sport should be grounded in an "inclusive" feminism, one that "utilizes multiple standpoints that take into account the intersections of class, race, gender, and other systems of domination and subordination'' (p. 136). He goes on to show through specific examples how to integrate analyses of masculinity with class, race, and sexual inequalities.

Is Feminist Cultural Studies the Answer?

Increasingly, and primarily in the United States, it is suggested that the theoretical underpinnings of a truly radical, gendered (and nonracialized) theory of sport lie in the combination of feminism and cultural studies. In this section I consider the possibilities and dangers of this liaison, and, more specifically, the implications for our theorizing and politicizing about gender and sport.

"What is cultural studies anyway?" asked Richard Johnson, a former director of the Centre for Contemporary Cultural Studies at the University of Birmingham in England. Fundamental to cultural studies is the importance of critique, and in Johnson's (1983) terms:

> I mean critique in the fullest sense: not criticism merely, nor even polemic, but procedures by which traditions are approached both for what they may yield and for what they may inhibit. Critique involves stealing away the more useful elements and rejecting the rest. It involves appropriation not just rejection. From this point of view cultural studies is a process, a kind of alchemy for producing really useful knowledge. Codify it and you might halt its reactions. (p. 9)

Cultural studies is a field in which different disciplines intersect in the analysis of *culture* defined as the "social forms through which human beings 'live,' become conscious, [and] sustain themselves subjectively" (Johnson, 1983, p. 24). Although it draws upon sociology, political science, philosophy, semiotics, history, literature, communication studies, and, more recently, feminism, it is antidisciplinary in the sense that cultural processes do not correspond to the contours of academic knowledge. According to Fred Inglis (1993), whose book charts the development of the field, cultural studies examines *culture in action*. A common misconception is that cultural studies is either limited to or primarily concerned with popular culture (e.g., television sitcoms, videos, rock music, romance novels, etc.). This is misleading for two reasons. First, all social practices including, for example, work, shopping, or childcare, can be looked at from a cultural point of view; and second, disciplines cannot begin to "do" cultural studies by simply expanding to encompass specific cultural forms, social groups, practices, or periods (Johnson, 1983; C. Nelson, Grossberg, & Treichler, 1992).

Another important aspect of cultural studies is the belief that its practice *does* matter, that there can be a bridge between theory and material culture, and that contemporary scholars can affect social change:

Every act of cultural struggle is thus not necessarily consistent with the politics of cultural studies, though cultural studies would agree with feminists, people of color, and those on the left that the canon presents a selective tradition that is deeply implicated in existing relations of power. (C. Nelson et al., 1992, p. 13)

Today, cultural studies and cultural theory are enjoying an international boom, especially in the United States, Britain, Australia, and less so in Canada; although its emphasis and projects are different depending upon the culture.[7] In some sense all versions have drawn their inspiration from British cultural studies, and the key institution was the Centre for Contemporary Cultural Studies at the University of Birmingham (founded in 1964, and now the Department of Cultural Studies). The writings of those who have been associated with the Centre both as staff and students still dominate the field (see Turner, 1990).

From the perspective of sport and leisure studies, however, we see a different pattern. Cultural studies has had more impact on the sociology of sport and leisure in Britain than in Canada and Australia, and much less influence on those areas in the United States. Those advocating a cultural studies/cultural criticism approach have challenged traditional mainstream approaches to sport sociology, and the debates have not been without rancor.[8] What these discussions clearly signal, as Peter Donnelly (1991) has noted, is a discernible shift from the traditional categoric and distributive research discussed in chapter 2 to a clearer understanding of what constitutes more theoretically informed analyses of social relations of power in sport and leisure. Sometimes omitted in these debates, but increasingly present, is the relationship between feminism and cultural studies and the potential of a cultural studies truly representative of all "difference."

Feminism and feminist theorizing were not part of the early work of the Centre for Contemporary Cultural Studies. It was through the efforts in the late 1970s of the Women's Studies Group at the centre (see *Women Take Issue*) that feminism forced a major reevaluation of every substantive area of work in cultural studies. Stuart Hall, who was Director of the Centre between 1969 and 1979, noted, "A theory of culture which cannot account for patriarchal structures of dominance and oppression is, in the wake of feminism, a non-starter" (S. Hall, 1980, p. 39). Later, he conceded that the intervention of feminism was specific, decisive, and ruptural (S. Hall, 1992). The early work on gender at the centre produced some excellent scholarship on women's leisure and girls' subcultures, which not only critiqued the consistent male bias of leisure studies and the sociology of youth but extended our knowledge about girls' and women's culture (Talbot, 1988).

Today, the influence of feminism on cultural studies is still limited, although certainly there is a recognition that both projects are concerned with, and wish to change, the forms and practices of power and inequality. If there are common goals between feminism and cultural studies, they are to investigate the role of culture in the reproduction of gender inequality and to ask how an analysis of gender can contribute to an understanding of culture (Franklin, Lury, & Stacey, 1991). But, as the editors of the second feminist anthology produced at the Birmingham Centre point out, "the models of culture employed within cultural studies have remained largely uninformed by feminist theories of patriarchy" (Franklin et al., 1991, p. 8). For example, the New Left theorizing (Marx, Althusser, Gramsci) upon which much of British cultural studies is based has been largely unable to account for sexuality, reproduction, and violence. Also, the notion of culture as "ways of life" and "ways of struggle" has often excluded the gendered dimensions of working-class experience; and the ethnographic work has been challenged for its lack of gender specificity.

Cultural studies also depends on an unexamined use of the concept "everyday" to ground its approach, but it is unclear precisely what is meant by the everyday since it can mean nearly anything; whereas in feminism, the everyday has been useful for an important oppositional critique, a site in which to locate difference and to expose the racial homogenization that continues within a gender analysis. Therefore, "the everyday becomes a figure for how disparity and division, rather than harmony and integrity, make up culture" (Langbauer, 1992, p. 125). Yet the "culture" of cultural studies means a whole way of life, that which is ordinary and located in the everyday, a homogenizing version of culture that *denies difference*. As I discuss in a later section, this is highly problematic for feminism.

Finally, within the institutional structures of higher education and the political movements outside these structures, where do feminism and cultural studies come together? Feminism is "practiced" primarily in three locations: in women's studies programs, which are now being institutionalized in universities in North America, Europe, and other areas of the world; in feminist theory, which is now being mainstreamed into the humanities and social sciences; and, most important, in the broader women's movement outside of academe. Cultural studies, on the other hand, remains almost exclusively within the academic setting but with relatively little institutionalization, and there is no particular political movement (outside the university) affiliated with cultural studies (Rooney, 1990). Feminist cultural studies, therefore, is far more likely to be happening in women's studies programs and in other departments (English is a prime site), which is fine as long as those programs also have an interest in sport and leisure. My experience is that women's studies programs in general have not embraced sport and leisure, nor have they been perceived as particularly inviting to physical education and sport studies students. My point here is that we need to think through the ramifications of where and how the building of a radical, gendered, and nonracist theory of sport will take place and by whom.

In the sections that follow, and in the next chapter, I explore some of the most recent work, primarily in the sociology of sport, that stems from a feminist cultural studies perspective. My discussion is neither as comprehensive nor as culturally diverse as it could be, but I hope it will give the reader a flavour of the type of work currently in progress. Sometimes it is useful to contrast this research and scholarship with that of other perspectives to clarify the potential advantages of feminist cultural studies and criticism. I also came to several conclusions about what needs to be emphasized at this particular juncture: the importance of more historically grounded studies; a sensitivity to difference, especially difference among women; the relationship of feminist theory to the study of men, sport, and masculinity; the significance of the body; and feminist cultural politics and sport. I address the first three areas in this chapter, the significance of the body in chapter 4, and the linkage between theory, politics, and practice in chapters 5 and 6.

The Importance of History

For sport historian Nancy Struna (1994), the task of the feminist social historian is to reconstruct the lives of real women who have had to negotiate a place for themselves within the repressive social relations of their time. Her work has focused on 17th- and 18th-century American colonial sport and, unlike traditional sport history, it portrays women as active agents in the construction of early American recreations. More generally, others have argued for feminist scholarship in sport history that moves away from "compensatory and contribution" history (vis-à-vis women) to a history that fully incorporates gender relations as an analytical category of historical research and redefines and expands concepts such as sport, competition, and women's culture (Parratt, 1994). In her comprehensive review of gender as a category of analysis within sport history over the last decade, Patricia Vertinsky (1994) offers the following assessment:

> The burgeoning scholarship in sport history and gender relations aims at much more than simply writing women into sport history. It seeks to forge new understandings of the historical relationship between sport and the social construction of gender by examining gender as a dynamic, relational process through which unequal power relations between women and men have been continually constructed and contested. (p. 23)

Some historians would argue further that a "new history" is emerging that recognizes women and minority groups, the lives of ordinary people, and the experiences of immigrants, lesbians and gay men, and people of color (Vertinsky, 1994). Feminist historians are now paying much more attention to feminist theory as they reconstruct women's vastly differing experience. Sport historians have been slower to take on board any theory, let alone feminist theory, but as Vertinsky's review makes clear, there is now a recognition by some that theory can inform the writing of history.

Historians of women's experience also acknowledge that women's sporting experience is a vastly underresearched area. Yet in the last few years there have appeared a number of superb dissertations from history students studying with well-known feminist historians, primarily in the United States. Their work is more sociologically grounded than earlier work in women's history, builds on the work of others, and represents a new approach to the study of women's sporting experience.[9]

For instance, Susan Cahn (1990, 1994) in a study of how gender and sexuality have been constructed within and through 20th-century women's sport in the United States uses several theoretical perspectives to inform her analysis. These perspectives include theories of cultural hegemony that focus on the ways in which sport reproduces the social structures and ideas of the dominant culture; feminist theories of the relationship between gender and sexuality that privilege the social and historical construction of this relationship over essentialist positions inherent in biology and psychology; and theories of cultural resistance in everyday life such as those found in British cultural studies, in gay and lesbian history and culture, and in poststructuralist theories of subjectivity about the way women call upon the multiple concepts and ideals of womanhood to negotiate the contradictions and difficulties of their subordinate status. None of these theoretical perspectives is adopted fully and uncritically, and as Cahn (1990) points out, "the body of the dissertation privileges the narrative over theoretical explications" (p. 13).

Cahn's narrative begins by examining early 20th-century debates in the United States about the development of sport and athletics in both middle- and working-class settings such as colleges, high schools, community centres, and industrial leagues. What becomes apparent is the struggle over competing philosophies of sport for girls and women led on the one hand by women physical educators who advocated programs of moderation and feminized versions of men's sports like girls' rules basketball, and on the other by the mostly male sponsors of popular, competitive women's events like the All-American Girls Baseball League who sought to feminize the athletes. Through her analysis, Cahn shows how sport organizations, principally in basketball, track and field, and softball/baseball, vied to control and define women's sport in the United States by constructing competing models of womanhood rooted in class-specific gender ideologies from the wider culture. She also pays considerable attention to the beginnings of women's sport, especially track and field, in African American communities, and, more important, how racism shaped women's sport in America.

Cahn takes her analysis deeper by looking more systematically at the gendering of sport, and, specifically, the boundaries between men's and women's activities, the concepts of masculinity and femininity, and the relative power of men and women. Through numerous examples and the oral history testimony of women athletes who competed in high-level competition between 1930 and 1970, she painstakingly describes how sport helped to construct the "gender order" (power relations between women and men) of 20th-century American society. Sport contributed to the fabrication of the gender order by "naturalizing" male dominance; preserving an arena of popular culture for men; dividing women along lines of class, race, and athletic interest; contributing to changes in gender ideologies in the dominant culture; and structuring physical and emotional experiences, and modeling the human body and human feeling around masculine and feminine axes. In tackling the difficult issues of lesbianism and homophobia in women's sport, Cahn traces the emergence of the lesbian stereotype in women's sport, the development of homophobia in women's physical education and sport, and the consequences for women both inside and outside of sport. Through oral histories of lesbian and nonlesbian athletes, she explores their subjective experience of the cultural association between sport and lesbianism.

We cannot fully explain the role of sport in the construction and persistence of unequal social relations today unless we understand the specific forms of these relations in the past and how they evolved over time. In her recent book, Jennifer Hargreaves (1994) provides a critical account, which is both historical and sociological, of the development of "sporting females" in Britain from the 19th century to the present day. "Time and time again," she argues, "the evidence suggests that female sports have been riddled with complexities and contradictions throughout their history" (p. 3). For instance, women opposed the popular notions of their biologically restricted bodies through their involvement into male-defined sport, but at the same time their physical emancipation was never without resistance, certainly from men. We need many more accounts of sporting females in a variety of cultures and historical periods before we can comprehend our past. At the same time, and without detracting from our need to understand gender subordination and oppression, it is also important to explore moments of escape and autonomy when women took pleasure in themselves, when they had fun. Jill Matthews, an Australian feminist historian, makes this point in her marvelous study of the Women's League of Health and Beauty, an exercise association whose heyday was in the 1930s when it boasted a membership of about 170,000 women in Britain, Australia, Canada, and Hong Kong. For many women, the league was where they made friends, took a night off, found a boyfriend (another league member's brother), and had a good deal of fun. Here then, argues Matthews (1990), "was a small space for women's pleasure that offered little challenge to the privileges and power of men and the heterosocial world" (p. 29).

Historical studies are extremely important because, as feminist cultural theorist Anne Balsamo (1994) asserts, they "illuminate the process whereby one set of beliefs (about female physiological inferiority) is articulated with another discursive system (concerning women's athletic practices)" (p. 343). For example, the historical scholarship of Patricia Vertinsky (1990) and Helen Lenskyj (1983, 1986), both of whom work in Canadian universities, describes yet another way in which women were discouraged from participating in sport through what we now understand to be culturally defined "facts" of the female body. These facts asserted that women were "eternally wounded" because they bled during part of their reproductive (menstrual) cycle. This popular myth—again supported by medical knowledge of the time—defined women as chronically weak and as victims of a pathological physiology. Two things happened here: Not only is the female body irrevocably tied to a culturally constructed obligation of reproduction, but also through the association between femininity and "the wound," the female body is coded as inherently pathological. Limiting women's participation in sport and exercise functioned both to control women's unruly physiology and to protect them for the important job of species reproduction. (Balsamo, 1994, p. 342-343)

Therefore, these historical analyses provide a useful way of understanding how the "natural" female body was taken up as a "cultural emblem of the reproductive body," (Balsamo, 1994, p. 343) with the consequence that women were often discouraged, and in some cases prevented, from participating in vigorous physical activity and thus fully experiencing their physicality.

A Sensitivity to "Difference"

Within feminist theory today, there are two opposing but related meanings of difference.[10] The first, often qualified as *sexual* difference, simply refers to the female/male dichotomy and the insistence that the male does not represent the universal. Women's experiences differ from those of men, something that until recently has not been fully recognized; women have actively participated in the construction of culture, and their participation is made visible by this use of difference. The second meaning of difference suggests difference or diversity in race, ethnicity, religion, class, sexuality, age, and disability *among women*. This meaning is related to the first because it has challenged not only notions of universal woman or women's experience, but also a homogeneous female voice. In sport-related research there has been much more emphasis placed on sexual difference and only some account taken of differences among women.

Sexual Difference

As I pointed out in chapter 2, categoric research, which is conducted primarily by psychologists, has focused on gender differences in sport and leisure and has explained these differences through biology or socialization. A major advance over this conceptualization is the now widespread understanding

that gender is a social and cultural construction. Sport historians have documented how the Victorian belief in innate biological and psychological differences between the sexes, perpetuated by the medical profession well into the
20th century, constructed woman as weak, inferior, and at the mercy of her
hormones, thereby justifying her exclusion from many sports and a strict
gender division in most others (Jennifer Hargreaves, 1994; Lenskyj, 1986;
Vertinsky, 1990). Sport sociologists have identified gender and gender difference as a social construction and have focused on the ways in which modern
sport is still used to construct and promote an ideology of natural gender
difference and the inferiority of women:

> The fact that no one can deny female difference becomes the fact of
> female sports inferiority, becomes the fact that females are innately
> different from men, becomes the fact that women who stray across
> the defining boundary are in a parlous state. An ideological view
> comes to be deposited in our culture as a common sense assump-
> tion—'of course women are different and inferior.' (P. Willis, 1982,
> p. 130)

The most visible and influential site for the promotion of sexual difference in sport is the media, and there is now an impressive collection of
critical media studies directed at "cracking the codes" through which the
media organize their (mis)representations of women's sport and make their
particular claims to common sense. The best of this work uses semiotics
(theory of signs and symbols), as well as critical feminist and cultural
theory, to examine the complex relationship between the "texts" (newspaper
accounts, television broadcasts, sports magazines, comic strips, advertisements, feature films, etc.), how ideologies are encoded in the texts, and how
these texts are "read" by those who consume them (audiences). The primary
focus of this work is on the "importance of discourses, representations,
and ideologies in naturalizing masculine dominance in sporting practices"
(McKay & Huber, 1992, p. 207).

Birrell and Theberge (1994a, pp. 346-356) provide an extensive survey
of this kind of research, primarily in North America. This research, they
suggest, demonstrates the absence or underrepresentation of women athletes
in the sport media and thus their "symbolic annihilation"; the trivialization
and marginalization of women athletes; the objectification and sexualization
or, more properly, heterosexualization of women athletes; the hidden discourse of homophobia in sport; the depiction of women's involvement in
sport as tragic; and the construction of women as unnatural athletes and
female athletes as unnatural women.

Similar themes are also apparent in the sports media outside North
America. In Britain, Jennifer Hargreaves provides an incisive critique of how
images of the female athlete are constructed and reproduced in children's
and adolescent weekly magazines, in newspapers, and on television. She

illuminates the link between the power of the images and the ideological, noting that these are not simply abstract ideas, since they constitute "a material force which permeates experience and is difficult to change" (Jennifer Hargreaves, 1994, p. 172).

Sport sociologist Jim McKay and his colleagues have analyzed current representations of the sporting woman in the Australian media. In one study (McKay & Huber, 1992) they show how media representations of sailing, specifically in commercial, 12-m yacht racing like the America's Cup, frame images of men's and women's bodies in ways that naturalize the technological and sporting superiority of men while at the same time marginalizing, containing, and incorporating visions of women. One important observation from their study is the need to understand women's complicity in reproducing these ideologies and why there is so little resistance to them. Thus the problem may not be one of sexual difference but rather the valorization and universalization of "male body experience," which both subsumes and devalues women. This led McKay and Huber to suggest that the important political task may be to "regender" rather than "degender"; in other words, it is important to restructure relations between men and women rather than completely removing gender as a category. Therefore, in the case of the media, by merely supplanting "false" images of female athletes with representations of "true sporting women," hegemonic male definitions of sport would go largely unchallenged.[11]

Jennifer Hargreaves (1993) has observed that "the body is a signifier of sexual difference and the ideology of gender difference the trademark of the sports media" (p. 60). She goes on to show, through specific examples from magazines, advertisements, photographs, and television images in the British media, how sport has become inextricably linked to both the commercialization of the female body and the commercialization of female heterosexualization. Similarly, Jim McKay (1994) shows how the "new" sporting woman is framed through the Australian media in "traditionally heterosexist and maternal narratives, while simultaneously intimating that they can be successful, enterprising *individuals*" (p. 79). The myth of the new sporting woman, McKay argues, naturalizes and depoliticizes power relations between women and men. We need more studies like these because they help expose the power of media representations to contain and naturalize women's sport and women athletes within the permissible spaces of sexual difference, female heterosexuality, and consumer culture.[12]

Differences Among Women

Canada, like many Western countries, is known as a "multicultural" society. For many decades there has been a steady decline in people of Anglo-Saxon heritage with a subsequent rise in the non-English and non-French population, now estimated at 30% of the total and comprising some 35 different cultural backgrounds. The majority of these ethnic minorities are European, with Asians, native peoples, and blacks constituting the racial minorities. Yet we know hardly anything about the role and significance of sport in various ethnic groups, male or female, either from the perspective of ethnocultural persistence or in the "making" of Canadians (M.A. Hall et al., 1991). We know virtually nothing about the role of sport and leisure in the lives of girls and women from established ethnic minorities or among recent immigrants. In Britain, Jennifer Hargreaves (1994, pp. 255-260) is able to draw on at least a small amount of investigative work specifically concerning Afro-Caribbean and southern Asian women, as well as her own interview material, but the lack of scholarship and consciousness about diversity remains. Sadly this reflects the very white bias of our scholarship, and we could make the same criticism of work in any multicultural society.

The sports world comprises the entire globe, and yet we constantly generalize from a Western, usually white, view of woman. Women's sport is not very globalized in that comparatively few women have the resources, time, and situations in which to participate, to recreate, or to compete. For example, participation and "success" (winning a medal) at the Olympic Games is highly concentrated among a few select countries, and there are many countries participating in the Olympics who send no women at all. In the 1988 Seoul Olympics, 42 of the 160 participating countries sent no women—mainly Asian and African nations that are predominantly Muslim. The Olympic winners come primarily from a tiny proportion of the participating countries. At Seoul 7 countries (East Germany, USSR, USA, Romania, Bulgaria, China, West Germany) won 8 out of 10 (79%) of all women's medals (Boutilier & San Giovanni, 1991). By my reckoning, these same countries accounted for somewhat fewer of the women's medals (58%) in the 1992 Barcelona Olympics due to the political changes in Eastern Europe, which have reunited the two Germanys but have severely curtailed the sport systems in state-socialist countries like Romania, Bulgaria, and Russia. The important point here is that, depending upon their circumstances, women's access to leisure and sport opportunities varies tremendously both within and among different cultures.

Sport sociologist Yevonne Smith (1992) has written that "before we can adequately build theory from a comprehensive womanist/feminist perspective, we must include the social realities of diverse ethnic females" (p. 246). She argues further that women of color[13] have historically been oppressed and omitted from the mainstream of society, sport, and scholarship; that they have been critical of exclusionary practices of white women scholars and of theory that treats them as invisible or as nonwomen; and that critical, relational analyses of the intersections of gender, race, and class are necessary. What Yevonne Smith, an African American, articulates is a critique voiced frequently by those who deplore the dominant white feminism and its academic expression in women's studies. Commenting upon the problems of feminist solidarity between white women and women of colour, bell hooks (1994, pp. 93-110) asserts that white feminists writing about difference and diversity do not make *their* lives, works, and experiences the subject of their analysis of race. Rather, she argues, white women still ignore the "relative absence of black women's voices, either in the construction of new feminist theory or at feminist gatherings" (p. 104).

Susan Birrell (1989, 1990) has brought some of this critique to the attention of a specifically sport sociology audience by exploring the challenge that the writings of women of colour pose to mainstream scholarship, race relations theory, feminist theory, and cultural studies. Their questioning has given rise to "identity politics," the belief that the most radical politics come directly out of our own identity (as a woman of colour, as a lesbian, as a woman with disabilities, as an old woman) rather than working to end the oppression of someone else's oppression. Alison Dewar (1993b) has argued that white, middle-class, heterosexual, and able-bodied women's experiences in sport are falsely universalized as representative of all women's experiences within the sports world. We must, she implores, give up theories that assume the existence of a "generic" sporting woman and develop work that reflects the diversity of all women's lives and their struggles against multiple oppressions. Her suggestions include not only retheorizing academic work, but also forming coalitions and alliances, and working together to learn how our experiences of oppression differ. As an example she suggests ways of challenging the dominance of heterosexuality in feminist sport sociology by refusing to marginalize and make invisible lesbian experience in sport.

What we have at present is some recognition of the divisions among sportswomen, such as those of class, race, religion, age, disability, and sexuality. But we also have very little understanding of how to undertake the retheorizing or how to develop universal political practices that go beyond the culturally specific. I discuss the latter point more in chapter 6. As for our scholarship, there are two major hurdles to overcome. One is that incorporating even some of the differences in women's sporting experiences is difficult because so much remains to be researched and written, but as more scholarship accumulates, it will become even more difficult unless we confront the problems of integration now (Gordon, 1991). Second, merely adding minority women's experience is not good enough; we must pay attention to relations among women and retheorize at the same time. Race, for example, cannot simply be added to existing theoretical frameworks. Race does not merely make the experience of women's oppression greater; rather it qualitatively changes the nature of that subordination (Maynard, 1990). Black sportswomen are not simply subjected to more disadvantages than their white counterparts; their oppression, because of racism, is qualitatively different in kind. At the very least, when we use the term "women's sporting experience" we need to be far more cognizant than we are at present of women's cultural and historical specificities. We also need to confront our own "isms" and reexamine our own practices.

Men, Sport, and Masculinity

I turn now to a brief examination of the developing scholarship about men's sport and masculinity, where similar issues arise because there are a multiplicity of masculinities—hegemonic, marginalized, and subordinated—and these also cut across differences of class, race, sexuality, and other social categories.

In the last decade, the sociological study of men and masculinity has emerged primarily in the United States, Australia, Britain, Canada, and parts of Europe as a new focus of attention among those concerned with gender. Conferences, books, and special journal issues all attest to this growing genre.[14] Obviously influenced by this broader work, there is now a growing number of predominantly male sport sociologists whose focus is the study of sport and masculinity, and, more specifically, the "male experience" in sport. The pioneers in this area are two Americans, Michael Messner and Donald Sabo, whose individual and collaborative work now spans 15 years. In their most recent collaboration, *Sex, Violence and Power in Sports: Rethinking Masculinity*, they tell their individual stories and of how they came to work together. Writing in this book on why the dialogue about men and masculinity is crucial, Don Sabo (1994) observes,

> It is critical in that it sees men and masculinity as a problem. It recognizes that there is something rotten in the ways that manhood has been defined, the ways that men spend their lives, and the ways that men relate to one another, to women, and the planet. Increasingly, men are beginning to reconsider their identities, their sexuality, and the violence they have shown toward women and toward one and another. A new area of writing and research, men's studies, not only seeks to critique men's lives, but to help men change themselves and reweave the latticework of their relationships with women and with one another. (pp. 194-195)

Although it is important to recognize the validity and importance of this relatively new work on masculinity, it is also important to acknowledge that a good deal of feminist analysis of sport, written by women, has also focused on men and masculinity. The explication of women's oppression and subordination *in* and *through* sport is totally bound up with the analysis of men and masculinity. In fact, as British sociologist Mary Maynard (1990) points out, "The literature written about women which has the most analytical depth is precisely that which has also included an analysis of male privilege and power" (p. 283). Therefore, studies conducted by men that will help women the most must go beyond merely investigating the male experience in sport and examine how male hegemony reproduces unequal gender relations. One example is the study of male bonding in the locker room whereby sexist and homophobic "talk fragments" are reinterpreted through a profeminist lens to reveal important assumptions about masculinity, male dominance, and fraternal bonding (Curry, 1991). Another example is a study of how in an Australian rural community men dominate local recreational resources and activities, and utilize women's domestic skills to facilitate their own public leisure, while at the same time deliberately excluding women from many of their activities (Dempsey, 1989, 1990). The work of Blye Frank (1993) and J.C. Walker (1988) in Canadian and Australian schools, respectively, on the development of masculinity and heterosexuality, the role of sport in male youth culture, and the implications for gender relations within educational settings is also worth noting. One final example is the analysis of sports violence as a social practice that helps to construct not only differences between various masculinities, but also the contemporary gender order of male dominance and female subordination (Messner, 1990a, 1992a).

In his evaluation of the growing scholarship on masculinity and sport, Mike Messner (1990b) argues, "It is precisely our experiences as men and our access to masculine worlds that gives us the potential to construct a powerful critique of masculinity" (p. 148). However, as he rightly points out, men should not trust their own experiences and ideas as the sole source of received knowledge; they must, in other words, "check with women." What this means is men must begin their analysis from explicitly feminist standpoints, avoid the universalization of men's experiences, examine critically intermale dominance hierarchies (e.g., gay and nongay, blacks and whites), and engage in studies that ultimately help us understand and change male privilege and power.

This chapter has focused primarily on theory, more specifically feminist cultural studies applied to sport. I have elaborated upon the meaning, potential, and dangers of the intersection between feminism and cultural studies as we move into a new era of theorizing about sport and gender relations. Although I have noted the importance of history, the need to be sensitive to sexual difference and to diversity among women, and the value of treating masculinity as problematic, I have not really shown what it means to "do" cultural studies. I do so in the next chapter, which focuses on the body, especially as it is being retheorized within an increasingly "corporeal" feminism.

Notes

1. This chapter is a revised and substantially edited version of M.A. Hall (1993).
2. Sport can be defined as the pursuit of a "non-utilitarian objective through engagement of bodily capacities and/or skills" (I.M. Young, 1979, p. 45). Sport sociologists, however, usually restrict their use of the term "sport" to institutionalized, formally organized sport. Not only is ice hockey, for example, in its institutionalized form(s) like the National Hockey League (NHL) more visible than children playing shinny on

ponds or corner rinks, but these formal institutions have the widest social effects and are, therefore, of the greatest sociological interest (see M.A. Hall et al., 1991, pp. 13-15, for more information).

3. Examples of these more critical texts are Sage (1990) in the United States; M.A. Hall et al. (1991) in Canada; McKay (1991), Rowe and Lawrence (1990), and Lawrence and Rowe (1986) in Australia; and John Hargreaves (1986) in Britain.

4. See also Jennifer Hargreaves (1994, pp. 12-24) for an excellent summary and critique of British sport sociology.

5. See note 1 at the end of chapter 2 for an explanation of Gramsci's theory of hegemony.

6. See also note 4 at the end of chapter 1.

7. For more information, see Brantlinger (1990); During (1993); Grossberg, Nelson, and Treichler (1992); Inglis (1993); Milner (1991); Nielsen and Morrow (1991); and Turner (1990).

8. For examples, see *Sociology of Sport Journal*, **4**, 1987; *International Review for the Sociology of Sport*, **26**, 1991; and, most recently, Rojek (1992), in addition to the special issue on British cultural studies in *Sociology of Sport Journal*, **9**, 1992.

9. See, for example, Helen Lenskyj, whose book *Out of Bounds* (1986) is a popularized and condensed version of her thesis completed at the Ontario Institute for Studies in Education under feminist theorist Mary O'Brien; Cindy Himes (now Gissendammer) (1986) who was supervised by Carroll Smith-Rosenberg at the University of Pennsylvania; Susan Cahn, whose book *Coming on Strong* (1994) is a rendering of her earlier thesis and who completed her work at the University of Minnesota under the supervision of Sara Evans; and Monys Ann Hagen (1990), whose work on the American industrial recreation movement and women's sports was supervised by Gerda Lerner at the University of Wisconsin-Madison.

10. In this paragraph, I am relying on Linda Gordon's (1991) superb essay on difference. There is obviously much more in her paper than I can mention here, and I strongly advise readers to see this for themselves. It serves as an excellent starting point to explore feminist theorizing around difference, particularly within the North American context.

11. McKay and Huber (1992) also predict that "we will never see a woman at the helm of an America's Cup yacht in this century" (p. 214). As I write this, one of the American contenders for the 1995 America's Cup competition is an all-female crew. Although I have not as yet seen any formal studies of the media representation of this event, the general theme in the popular press is predictably along the lines of whether the "girls" are actually strong enough to beat the "boys," and although they may be strong enough, they really are "nice" girls, and of course very feminine (see, for example, Karbo, 1995).

12. Obviously the role of the media in constructing sexual difference, and indeed the relationship of the media to women's sport in general, is a huge topic deserving much more attention than I have paid it here. For a useful, although somewhat traditional approach to the larger topic, see Creedon (1994).

13. By "women of color," Yevonne Smith (1992) means several diverse ethnic groups: African American, Hispanic (Latino, Puerto Rican, Chicano), Asian American (Korean, Chinese, Japanese, Vietnamese), or Native American (Indian, Alaskan Native, Hawaiian Islander).

14. For an excellent review of several recent books about "men's experience," see Kimmel (1992); for more academic material on research about "masculinities," see the special issue of *Theory and Society*, **22** (5), 1993, edited by Robert W. Connell.

The Significance of the Body

4   The academic discipline and professional practice known as physical education, at least in North America, has curiously disembodied the very focus of its discourse, *the body*. Exercise biochemists study individual bodily cells; exercise physiologists investigate single muscle groups or bodily parts; biomechanists explore the physical principles of bodily movement; human motor behaviourists research body memory and perception; and sport psychologists work on the head. In this rational, scientific view, the body is an objective entity to be dissected, manipulated, treated, improved, and utilized as an instrument for achievement. Even the sociology of sport until recently has ignored the body, in preference to studying the structural, institutional, economic, and cultural aspects of sport. Bodies themselves are generally left to those subfields that deal with them rationally, albeit piecemeal, like anatomy, physiology, biomechanics, and sports medicine.

Bodies in the 1990s, however, have become central to academic discourse in the humanities, although perhaps less so in the social sciences. There is, for example, now a growing literature on the sociology of the body, some of which has been influenced by feminist theory. Arthur Frank's (1991) comments are particularly insightful here:

The sociology of the body understands embodiment not as residual to social organization, but rather understands social organization as being about the reproduction of embodiment. Embodiment is anything but a neutral constant in social life, representing instead the political principles of class and gender domination. On the questions of domination and appropriation hang much of the story of society. Feminism has taught us that that story both begins and ends with bodies. (p. 42)

Few today would dispute the need for a fully embodied sociology of sport to counter a legacy of disembodied sociological discourse about society, sport, and culture.[1] Although feminism is usually recognized as contributing to this discourse, feminism itself is often treated as if it were a singular and coherent body of theory. I hope it is clear to the reader by now that nothing could be further from the truth. Therefore, my primary aim in this chapter is to explain not only the varied responses within feminism to women's bodily specificity but also how feminists have sought to theorize the sexualized or gendered body. I also illustrate the "doing" of feminist cultural studies through two relatively new sites of women's sporting and exercising bodies, namely, aerobics and bodybuilding. I conclude with some thoughts on where all this leads us in terms of future research.

Feminism and Sporting Bodies

Female bodies have always been central to feminism, but sporting bodies have not. As a social movement, second-wave feminism has been responsible for raising consciousness about the exploitation and control of women's bodies. Feminists have fought hard to put sexual harassment and abuse, domestic violence and rape, pornography and advertising, medical interventions and reproductive technology on public and political agendas. A major feminist demand is that women have the right to control their bodies and to make choices in their interests, not those of men or the state. However, feminists have rarely paid attention to female *sporting* bodies, nor have they always seen the relevance of physicality, or empowerment through physical activity, to feminist politics.

Within feminism there have been primarily two responses to women's corporeal or bodily specificity (Caddick, 1986; Gatens, 1992).[2] One argues for sexual equality regardless of biological differences, and the other celebrates and retains an essential sexual difference. On the sexual equality side are those who assert that the specificity of the reproductive (woman's) body must be overcome, through scientific intervention if necessary, for equality with men to be achieved. Certainly sport has been a prime site for the intervention into women's bodies and their reproductive capacity through a variety of measures to maximize performance, such as the deliberate post-ponement of puberty or the control of menstruation through the administration of hormones and the taking of performance-enhancing drugs.

On the other side are those who argue that there is an essential sexual difference between men and women that should be retained and celebrated, not eroded by scientific intervention. Women, in other words, should not aspire to be "like men" (Gatens, 1992). There is, of course, a long tradition of "sport-for-women" in North America and Britain, and other countries as well, based precisely on this premise.[3] Thirty years ago, American physical educator Eleanor Metheny (1965) argued that the so-called irreconcilability between feminine desirability and athletic prowess had its origin in some "biologically-defined difference common to men and women of all social groups," even though she recognized that this notion worked as a powerful social sanction (p. 52). More recently, longtime observer and scholar of women's sport Carole Oglesby called the contributors to *Sport, Men, and the Gender Order* to task for not recognizing the "feminine force" in sport, which she characterized as passive, subordinate, cooperative, dependent, chaotic, nonviolent, and nurturant (Oglesby, 1990). The natural antidote to the "androgen poisoning" prevalent in today's sports world, she argued, is a good dose of the "elements of the traditional feminine" (p. 242). By androgen poisoning, I assume Oglesby means that modern-day women's sport, and indeed much of men's traditional sport, has been contaminated by so-called male values such as aggression, competition, achievement, and violence, and it has ignored the more genteel principles encompassed in sport-for-women.

At the heart of this sexual difference versus sexual equality debate, and therefore with essentialism and biological determinism on the one hand and social constructionism on the other, is the problematic framework of Western philosophical dualisms[4]—body/mind, nature/culture, emotion/reason, private/public—since both positions seek to privilege one side of the dualism over the other (Gatens, 1992). Most feminist theorists have been extremely wary of these dualisms because they frequently lend themselves to the positioning of woman as opposite to, and the negation of, man. Western culture tends to associate women with bodies/nature/emotion/private and men with the more valued mind/culture/reason/public, thus trapping women in their bodies as "natural." For example, as I discuss in chapter 3 (see pp. 40-42) the most visible and influential site for the promotion of sexual difference in sport is the media, which work to "naturalize" differences between male and female athletes. To put this another way and to generalize to other cultural practices,

instead of granting women an autonomous and active form of corpo-real specificity, at best women's bodies are judged in terms of a "natural inequality," as if there were a standard or measure for the value of bodies independent of sex. In other words, women's corpo-real specificity is used to explain and justify the different (read:

unequal) social positions and cognitive abilities of the two sexes. By implication, women's bodies are presumed to be incapable of men's achievements, being weaker, more prone to (hormonal) irregularities, intrusions, and unpredictabilities. (Grosz, 1994, p. 14)

Yet feminist theorists have not always been successful in escaping these dualisms, especially when thinking about women's bodies. Some radical feminist thinkers (e.g., Mary Daly) simply reversed the dualisms by placing more value on the "feminine" and hence the body, nature, emotion, the private sphere, and so forth. As a result, they have been accused of embracing essentialism and critiqued by those espousing a social constructionist position, including most feminist sport scholars, who stress ideology, cultural values, and power relations. Today, feminist theorists are tackling head on the reluctance among some to conceptualize the female body as playing a major role in women's oppression.

Australian feminist philosopher Elizabeth Grosz, who has contributed significantly to the articulation of a "corporeal feminism," argues that so far bodies have been theorized as either anatomical, physiological, or biological, thus obscuring the possibility of sociocultural conceptions of the body (Grosz, 1991, 1993, 1994). Her work is part of the larger feminist challenge, inspired by postmodernism, to the underlying assumptions of knowledge production, particularly in the humanities and social sciences. This "crisis of reason," as referred to by some, is an attack on the very dualisms of Western philosophical thought I discussed earlier, indeed on all of Western reason. In Grosz's words,

> Philosophy has surreptitiously excluded femininity, and ultimately women, from its practices through its usually implicit coding of femininity with unreason associated with the body. It could be argued that philosophy as we know it has established itself as a form of knowing, a form of rationality, only through the disavowal of the body, specifically the male body, and the corresponding elevation of mind as a disembodied term." (1994, p. 4)

Grosz (1994) proposes how a different analysis of the body might proceed, and she outlines several goals and criteria she believes should govern a feminist theoretical approach to concepts of the body. The approach must avoid the impasse of the mind/body dualism by developing an understanding of "embodied subjectivity" or "psychical corporeality." No one body can be the model for all others; there must be a plurality of body types—young and old, black and white, male and female—and one cannot function as the representative of another. Biologism and essentialist accounts of the body must be avoided, and the body regarded as a site of social, political, cultural, and geographical inscriptions (see discussion in chapter 2, pp. 13-18). Finally, and this is her most provocative statement, "the body is neither—while also being both—the private or the public, self or other, natural or cultural, psychical or social, instinctive or learned, genetically or environmentally determined'' (1994, p. 23). Therefore, in order to avoid social constructionism, the body's "nature" can be invoked, yet in opposing essentialism, biologism, and naturalism, it is the body as a cultural product that must be stressed. It is in this sense that Grosz sees bodies as having all the explanatory power of minds.

I return to some of these notions later in the chapter and attempt to show their relevance to female sporting and exercising bodies. Before doing so, however, it is useful to examine briefly the work of French theorist Michel Foucault on feminist theorizing about bodies because his influence has been profound.

The Influence of Michel Foucault

What interests feminists most is the *sexualized* or *gendered* body, which brings together a convergence of recent developments in feminist thought, postmodernist theory, and the development of a critical sociology of the body (Morgan & Scott, 1993). Feminists have been particularly attracted to the work of Michel Foucault because of his insistence on the body as an historical and culturally specific entity, thus providing a way to conceive of the sexualized body without positing an original sexual difference or fixed biological essence (McNay, 1991). As Moira Gatens (1992) puts it, "It is important to create the means of articulating historical realities of sexual difference without thereby reifying these differences" (p. 130).

Foucault's writings also highlight how bodies are constructed through a variety of *discourses*, such as medical, scientific, technological, sexual, and sporting. The meaning of discourse in this sense is "the structured ways of knowing which are both produced in, and the shapers of, culture" (Ransom, 1993, p. 123). Theorists like Foucault, and others who are labeled postmodernist or poststructuralist, stress the importance of language and representation, the principle ingredients of any discourse.[5] Discourses, however, are not merely linguistic phenomena but are always "shot through" with power and are institutionalized as practices. For example, within the sport discourse, there are disputes about the essence of sport and about the defining characteristics (e.g., the complexity and variety of physical skills required) that allow particular activities to be classified as sports. However, these controversies are much less important than the social relations and distribution of political and economic resources that have meant that some games and physical pursuits have become institutionalized features of a particular culture while others have not (M.A. Hall et al., 1991).

As Gruneau (1993, p. 102) argues, it does not take much imagination to suggest what a Foucauldian analysis of modern sporting and exercise practices might look like: the values of discipline, health, and self-improvement could be seen as interiorized in the body in ways that support powerful new forms of docility and normalization; the discourses of sports promoters and health and physical education professionals are an essential part of the emerging technology of normalization; the changing nature of training regimes and relationships between athletes, coaches, and administrators are at times based on surveillance; and so on. However, as Andrews (1993) points out in his analysis of how Foucault's understanding of the human body is linked to a critical discourse within sport sociology, very few sport theorists have properly utilized his insights.

Such is not the case within feminism where there is now a vigorous, if not contentious, engagement with Foucault.[6] The attraction as mentioned previously has been largely because Foucault places the human body at the centre of the historical struggle between different power formations. Monique Deveaux (1994), in a critical analysis of feminists' appropriation of Foucault, suggests that there are three "waves" of Foucauldian scholarship produced by feminist political theorists and philosophers. These are: (a) literature that appropriates Foucault's analysis of the effects of power on bodies; (b) analyses that expand upon Foucault's later and more complex understanding of power, which allowed for some notion of "resistance"; and (c) postmodern feminist writings on sexual and gender identity informed by Foucault's account of the proliferation of discourses on sex in the modern era.[7]

The first wave appropriates Foucault's analysis of the effects of power on bodies, more concisely known as the "docile bodies" thesis. In *Discipline and Punish*, Foucault argued that the transition from traditional to modern societies has been characterized by a profound transformation in the exercise of power. No longer embodied in the person of the monarch and exercised upon a largely anonymous body of subjects, power in modern society is more insidious and subtle, requiring self-surveillance. For example, Sandra Bartky (1988, p. 71), in her essay on the social construction of femininity, identifies some of the "technologies of femininity" such as dieting and exercise regimes aimed at attaining the "ideal" body, as well as the whole range of gestures, postures, movements, and bodily comportments that restrain women. She then shows how these technologies of femininity are "taken up and practised by women against the background of a pervasive sense of bodily deficiency" (1988, p. 71). Susan Bordo provides another example of the appropriation of Foucault's docile bodies paradigm through his notion of self-surveillance. In a series of essays (now collected in her book *Unbearable Weight*), Bordo (1993) explores "the cultural representations of female hunger and female eating, the role of consumer culture, long-standing philosophical and religious attitudes toward the body, similarities to other predominantly female disorders (agoraphobia, hysteria), connections with other contemporary body obsessions, continuities with 'normal' female experience in our culture, and so forth" (p. 32). She states that Foucault's notion of power has been extremely helpful both to my analysis of the contemporary disciplines of diet and exercise and to my understanding of eating disorders as arising out of and reproducing normative feminine practices of our culture, practices which train the female body in docility and obedience to cultural demands while at the same time being *experienced* in terms of power and control. (p. 27)

Another example of this first wave appropriation is the work of Jennifer Terry on the medical surveillance of women as reproducers through regulatory prenatal technologies (e.g., amniocentesis, sonograms, electronic fetal monitoring), which allow the state (through medical authorities) to view the fetus as separate from the mother. The Foucauldian notion being appropriated here is that of "biopower," which describes the state's relatively new interest in the birth rate, education, discipline, health, and longevity of its population. In an essay about women's sporting bodies, Cheryl Cole (1993) argues that "surveillance-dominated capitalism," a product of right-wing American politics, obscures the context in which the body and exercise have become commodified in ways that "manage" gender relations. The notion of surveillance, the idea that individuals will be constantly monitored and under observation, is taken directly from Foucault who saw the characteristic forms of power in the modern prison (or by extension in factories, schools, offices, organisations) as discipline and surveillance. Cole shows how routine, invasive surveillance practices—drug testing and blood tests (for AIDS) of all athletes, mandatory sex and pregnancy testing of female athletes, and the potential of genetic engineering to improve the athletic body—labeled "body McCarthyism" by some, have been legitimated by the state of which the "sport-apparatus" is a part.

As Deveaux (1994) points out, the major critique of these feminist appropriations utilizing the docile bodies and biopower constructs has been the unquestioned acceptance of Foucault's monolithic, unidirectional notion of power with its inexorable and repressive grip on its subjects. The consequence of this undifferentiated account of power is that he fails to elaborate any notion of resistance on the part of those subject to disciplinary power (McNay, 1991). It also reflects Foucault's tendency to understand subjects as docile bodies rather than as individuals or persons, and what his work cannot explain is how "women simply do not slip easily and passively into socially prescribed feminine roles" (McNay, 1992, p. 135).

Foucault's later works gave way to a more complex understanding of power that recognized that individuals contest fixed identities and relations in ongoing and sometimes subtle ways. Deveaux (1994) argues that this formulation of "where there is power, there is resistance" characterizes the second wave of feminist appropriation of Foucault, and she cites the work of several feminist philosophers, including Nancy Fraser and Nancy Hartsock, who have engaged this notion of power. Sport sociologist Nancy Theberge (1987), in her essay on sport and women's empowerment, utilizes Hartsock's reconceptualization of power, which stresses energy and creativity rather than strength and domination. Theberge argues that "the liberatory possibility of sport lies in the opportunity for women to experience the creativity and energy of their bodily power and to develop this power in the community of women" (p. 393). Yet Deveaux is skeptical, arguing that Foucault's agonistic model of power is double-edged: It disengages us from simplistic, dualistic accounts of power; but at the same time, it obscures many important experiences of power specific to women and fails to provide a sustainable notion of agency. She suggests that feminists "need to look at the *inner* processes that condition women's sense of freedom or choice in addition to external manifestations of power and dominance" (1994, p. 234).

Where does this leave us with regard to the appropriation of Foucauldian concepts for feminist ends? Deveaux argues that a feminist analysis of power would avoid the omissions and problems of Foucault's understanding of power in four key ways. First, it would avoid the pitfalls of a static docile bodies paradigm of subjectivity. It would do this by "conceptualizing women's relationship to their bodies as both a reflection of social construction *and* of their own responses to (and mediation of) the cultural ideals of femininity" (1994, p. 244). Second, it would attend to the myriad sources of disempowerment and oppression experienced by women by rejecting aspects of Foucault's agonistic model of power. Third, it would take seriously the issue of women's empowerment, their capacities for self-determination and freedom, and the conditions in which these flourish. Fourth, it would dispute the postmodern feminist assertion that the category "women" be displaced from the centre of feminist politics.

I have spent some time outlining the use being made of Foucault by feminist theorists of the body, as well as the dangers in doing so, because there are some important applications to be made to theoretically informed analyses of women's sporting and exercising bodies. Some work in this area is beginning to appear in the literature, and one assumes that there will be more to follow. In the next section, I focus on a form of "mass" exercise that women have taken up in ever increasing numbers since the 1960s, namely, aerobics. Then, in the section that follows, I discuss much more transgressive body work taken up by women, specifically, bodybuilding. Both are useful sites for the kind of theorizing, stemming mainly from feminist cultural studies, that helps us understand, analyze, and critique these contested terrains of women's physicality and work out effective feminist political practices.

Theorizing Women's Sporting/Exercising Bodies

How are we to make sense of the phenomenal changes in women's sport and exercise participation in North American culture since the early 1960s? Susan Willis (1990) observes that "many young women today do not realize that exercise for women as a widely available and socially acceptable endeavor represents a recent victory in women's struggle for equality with men'' (p. 3). She also notes that women today set vastly different exercise standards for themselves than did women 20 and 30 years ago. Daily 60-min aerobic workouts, jogging programs covering 30 to 50 km a week, strenuous athletic training regimes for women with disabilities, and challenging exercise programs for seniors all attest to the increased capabilities and interests among exercising women, albeit still a very small proportion (mainly white, middle-class, and professional) of the total population.

Feminist analyses of women's "exercising bodies" have primarily centered on aerobics as the site of the exercise. Perhaps most important is the theme that appears over and over again: how to reconcile the public discourse of aerobics, which I will discuss in a moment, with an individual "aerobicizer's" subjective understanding of her activity and her body. Pirkko Markula, a Finnish researcher who completed her dissertation at the University of Illinois, illustrates the problem when she says,

> The public discourses surrounding aerobics evidently emphasize a fragmented view of self by focusing overtly or covertly on improving one's body shape. Aerobicizers' relationships to their selves, however, prove to be contradictory: fragmented in attempts to conform with the societal ideal body image, but yet integrated in the enjoyment of movement. It became obvious in my research that the individual women in exercise classes actively create meanings of their selves, but these meanings continue to be framed and constructed by the dominant forces in society. Women seek their full potential and empowerment in the integration of self in aerobics, but at the same time desire to conform with the societal construction of the ideal feminine body. Evidently, women are neither merely objects of the invisible oppressive power, as Foucauldian theory might suggest, nor subjects, free from any control, to make their own meanings in society. (Markula, 1993, p. 98)

Other cultural theorists have expanded on the public discourses that surround aerobics. One of the first was Margaret Morse (1988) in a fascinating article about the "media complex of exercise," specifically televised exercise programming in the United States (e.g., *The Richard Simmons Show*, *Jane Fonda's Workout*) now readily available on video cassette. Morse argues that aerobics, an activity that spans the cultural categories of sport, dance, and exercise, has become the latest commodity in the highly commercialized beauty culture:

> Exercise can be added to the applications of makeup and clothing and to the body-moulding regimes of corseting, diet, and surgical intervention (including plastic surgery and lipo-suction) as a means of achieving femininity. Of these methods, exercise was one of the

first brought in service to a feminist alternative ideal of the female body and one of the last to be commercialized, perhaps because of the intrinsic properties the activity possesses. Rather than applying "a second skin" of femininity externally, both diet and exercise work from the inside out, requiring an assertion of will over the body. But while dieting shrinks the body and its power both literally and symbolically, exercise prepares a freely-moving subjectivity which can be active in the world. As such it contradicts long-prevailing notions of feminine passivity and stasis. (p. 24)

Calling on an array of theorists as diverse as Jean Baudrillard, Jacques Lacan, Victor Turner, Erving Goffman, and Hannah Arendt, Morse proceeds to "deconstruct" these exercise videos by examining the cultural forms (e.g., the mirror construction) embodied in aerobics, the social relations within the aerobic realm, and the possibility of aerobics as a "transitional cultural form." She ends by suggesting three possible feminist strategies aimed at changing the "aerobics invention." First, a kinder, more variable, and more forgiving ideal of femininity needs to be constructed. Second, bodily activity should be redesigned to incorporate interaction among participants rather than the simultaneous mirroring so characteristic of aerobic classes. Finally, where masculine imagery has the power to represent men of any age, race, build, or social status, and even a whole nation (think of football in the United States and ice hockey in Canada), women are held to the "literalness of embodiment." By changing the imagery, there is the potential to have self-action in women's bodies, rather than have them remain a site of obsession.

The fitness "workout" is an example of the contradictory synthesis of work and leisure. In her cultural critique of "working out," Susan Willis (1990) examines aerobics, as well as exercising on Nautilus equipment. She argues that the workout "may well represent the most highly evolved commodity form yet to appear in late-twentieth-century consumer capitalism" (p. 6). The workout also represents the culmination of a trend toward privatization in the exercise culture: for example, exercising at home to a television program or video or better still having a personal trainer visit your home. Specific to women, the workout focuses "their positive desires for strength, agility, and the physical affirmation of self and transforms these into competition over style and rivalry for a particular look and performance" (p. 7). By wearing their workout costumes in public, women can make a public statement about having "seized control over the making and shaping" (p. 7) of their bodies.

Most of the work I have been discussing so far is based on an analysis of the "texts" (e.g., television programs, videos, books) of the aerobics phenomenon, all of which help to define the public discourse. I want to return, however, to Markula's (1993) observation, based on her ethnographic research, that women's subjective voices "play an important role in resisting the prevailing discourses which tend to assign women to inferior positions in society'' (p. 93). Based on extensive interviews and participant observations of female aerobicizers, she found that although women work hard to attain the ideal body—lean, healthy, youthful—they take enormous pleasure in achieving this outcome. Aerobics is also a source of self-confidence and self-esteem for women, which means (although she has no real evidence to support this) that women can free themselves from the controlling images of femininity. Finally, her respondents indicated that they felt increased energy following an aerobics workout, suggesting a more integrated sense of self.

The important point to be made here is that cultural analyses based solely on public discourse or texts, without also exploring the meaning of these discursive practices to those who participate in them, provides a one-sided, probably inaccurate, picture of the activity or cultural form. I return to this issue in the next section on women's bodybuilding.

Resistance and Compliance: The Case of Women's Bodybuilding

Women's bodybuilding, both as a sport and a subculture, has grown rapidly since the early 1980s along with mass media and fan attention.[8] In the United States, there have been competitive women's bodybuilding contests since 1979, and on a more casual level, increasing numbers of women have taken up weightlifting as part of general exercise and fitness programs.[9] For men, bodybuilding appears to fulfill a need, through the creation of a virile, hyper-masculine physique, to restore feelings of self-worth and self-control (Gillet & White, 1992; Klein, 1993). For women, however, it is much more difficult to attribute a singular goal or meaning, and it may be possible to represent women's bodybuilding in one of two ways. On the one hand, Grosz (1994) argues that it may be part of an attempt to conform to stereotypical images of femininity, ''a form of narcissistic investment in maintaining her [hetero-sexual] attractiveness to others and herself'' (p. 224). On the other hand, it can be seen as an attempt ''to take on for herself many of the attributes usually granted only to men—strength, stamina, muscularity—in a mode of defiance of patriarchal attempts to render women physically weak and incapable'' (p. 224). Therefore, bodybuilding for women can be seen both as a form of compliance to the requirements of femininity and as a mode of resistance to those same requirements. Women's bodybuilding is, according to bodybuilder and anthropologist Anne Bolin (1992b), ''saturated with contradiction.''

Research and scholarship about women's bodybuilding are prevalent in three areas. First, there is the social psychological research around the perceptions and self-images of female bodybuilders, which not surprisingly shows that females are viewed negatively in "gender-inappropriate" sports like competitive bodybuilding.[10] Second, there is an increasing number of ethnographic studies of both the elite, competitive, and often professional bodybuilders (known as the "hard-core") and the more casual bodybuilder whose reasons for participating and training are for fitness, health, appearance, and self-esteem. Third, there are the complex and sophisticated feminist cultural analyses and critiques that usually focus on the texts of bodybuilding, such as magazines, photos, videos, and film. I will concentrate on the second and third of these areas—the ethnographic and the cultural criticism—and how the two interrelate.

The female bodybuilder, argues cultural theorist Laurie Schulze (1990), is difficult to position within any existing "cultural map of the feminine" because she is a "direct, threatening resistance to patriarchy at its most biologist foundations" (p. 71). What Schulze means here is that the female bodybuilder threatens not only current socially constructed definitions of femininity and masculinity, but the system of sexual difference as well: "The deliberately muscular woman disturbs dominant notions of sex, gender, and sexuality, and any discursive field that includes her risks opening up a site of contest and conflict, anxiety, and ambiguity" (p. 59). Popular discourse today, at least in North America, invokes a normative ideal of female beauty that is slim, strong, sinuous, athletic, and healthy. There is no question that this particular female body type has become a marketable commodity, and the fitness-related industries, including equipment and sportswear manufacturers, magazine publishers, television program producers, and people like self-anointed fitness guru Susan Powter have profited enormously. The professional female bodybuilder, Schulze argues, is placed either at the limits of the ideal or just beyond its boundaries, and is often characterized in terms of "excess." If she transgresses the ideal, there is "an attempt to ease her back into the space secured by the ideal, emphasizing certain features, suppressing others, and papering over contradictions" (p. 61).

Professional bodybuilder Bev Francis is a good case study of this process of transgression and resistance, followed by compliance.[11] I remember my astonishment when I first caught a glimpse of her incredibly powerful and muscular body on a television talk show in the early 1980s. I had never before seen someone so clearly a woman, yet in a "man's body." In 1984 she appeared as one of the principal characters in the movie *Pumping Iron II: The Women*, which chronicles the 1983 Caesar's World Cup Competition, one of the early women's bodybuilding contests. A former powerlifter, the Australian Francis was pitted against more conventionally feminine (prettier, sexier, less bulky, more curvaceous) competitors, and she did not fare well; in fact, she placed last among the eight finalists. According to the judges, she lacked the appropriate amount of "aesthetic femininity," and worse, she had taken female musculature to excess (Holmlund, 1989). She was, in their view, a "she-man" (Ian, 1991). Yet 4 years later Bev

Francis won the Women's Pro World Championship, and from 1987 through 1991 she placed either second or third in the prestigious Ms. Olympia contest. Her original 180-lb, bulky size was considerably reduced to the right proportion of muscularity and symmetry, she wore makeup and fluffed her bleached blond hair, she had cosmetic surgery on her nose, and she appeared in nifty, colour-coordinated (usually pink) posing bikinis and Spandex outfits (Bolin, 1992a). Her transformation from the "woman in the man's body" to just the right amount of musculature with the appropriate feminine comportment was complete, and so too was her ability to market herself and her new body. Bev Francis is the most obvious case of what Schulze identifies as the strategies to "tame" professional female body-builders and make sense of their bodies by pulling them back toward a normalizing regime. Their heterosexuality and heterosexual desirability are secured, their muscle is rephrased as "flex appeal" and shows only when "pumped up," and their bodies are positioned as the site of heterosexual pleasure, romance, youth, fun, and beauty.

However, an analysis centered solely on the texts or discourse of female bodybuilding begs the question of why it is so troubling and why it attracts these strategies in the first place. Although strategies of domination operate to control meaning, they can be opposed by the production of counterideologies, which led Schulze to conclude that her work was incomplete without an ethnographic study of female bodybuilding subcultures to investigate the meanings and pleasures made by its members, as well as by its audiences. Such studies are now appearing more frequently in the literature.

Anthropologist Anne Bolin, who is herself a competitive bodybuilder, has probably been in the best position to unravel the complexities of the female bodybuilding subculture. Through participant-observer studies in the locker-room society of hard-core gyms, participation in health clubs and spas, interaction with training partners, and her own preparation for and participation in bodybuilding contests, she has been able to travel inside the world of the competitive female bodybuilder. Her project, which is informed by feminist theory and postmodernism as well as symbolic and interpretive anthropology, is to describe and interpret the actual practices of competitive bodybuilding. In one study she examined the role of dieting and nutrition in shaping the bodybuilders' physiques—their training diets, precontest regimes, and the bingeing on forbidden foods after a contest— showing how men and women bodybuilders differ in their approach to food and fat (Bolin, 1992a). Where men worry that their diet will "eat up their muscle" and make them look small, women fret that they will not appear "hard" and firm enough, and that if they appear "soft," it indicates the presence of fat deposits over the muscle. As women lose fat, however, they also forfeit the cultural insignias of sexual difference (e.g., breast fat) meaning that male and female bodies become increasingly similar.[12] Many female bodybuilders opt for surgical breast implants to try to salvage an aspect of their femininity (Ian, 1991). Contradictorily, both sexes must become much leaner in order to appear more dense and muscular. In another paper Bolin explores the question of "how much beast can be tolerated in the beauty" by showing through an analysis of judging criteria how muscular symmetry has come to denote femininity:

> But the woman bodybuilder cannot follow the "masculine" imperative too far, for she must maintain a seemingly ineffable quality of "femininity" that is never defined or clearly articulated. This is indeed one of the few sports that a competitor can be too good; she can have too much muscle. (Bolin, in press, p. 16)

This led former competitive bodybuilder Marcia Ian (1991, p. 4) to ask, "In what other sport could a female competitor be expected to limit her achievement for fear of losing her proper gender?" Therefore, these ethnographic studies confirm Schulze's notion that transgression or excess is always pulled back through compliance to the "norms" of femininity. As Bolin (in press) observes, whereas the "beast" challenges male privilege, the "beauty" sustains it.

As I pointed out earlier, women's competitive bodybuilding is a relatively new sport, which means that women have invaded a cultural area previously defined as exclusively male. In another interesting ethnographic study, sociologists Leslie Miller and Otto Penz (1991) analyze how "power struggles over sites in the sociocultural landscape always involve struggles over *meaning*" (p. 149). Through conversations with female bodybuilders who train in commercial and campus gyms in a western Canadian city, Miller and Penz examined the discursive strategies female bodybuilders employed to make a place for themselves in a male sport through the negotiation of meaning. They found that the women defined bodybuilding as a "sport of appearance" in the sense that managing one's appearance is specifically women's body work. The women also attempted to disentitle men's claim to the field by asserting that certain male uses of bodybuilding (for ego, as an example) were inappropriate. Finally, the women saw their own bodywork, the sort of work at which women excel, as not necessarily in the service of male interests, but as able to be put to good use in the service of female mastery and control. On the strategic and practical level, the women's claim was roughly, "They [men] don't really understand the nature of bodybuilding; their masculinity gets in the way" (p. 157). The women bodybuilders in this study reclaimed the best-at-bodywork rhetoric and turned it to their advantage and in this way were able to stake a new claim for themselves in a formerly masculine preserve. This is a good example of the sort of counterideological production discussed on a theoretical level by Schulze.

The final area of study of women's bodybuilding concerns the question of audience or spectator reaction to the sport. Annette Kuhn's (1988) perceptive analysis of the film *Pumping Iron II: The Women* demonstrates the value of feminist film theory to a cultural analysis of women's sport and women's bodies.[13] In this case, the audience was primarily a feminist one who reacted inconsistently with much enjoyment during the screening, but afterwards with negative criticism directed at female bodybuilding. Kuhn suggests that the audience was uncomfortable with its own pleasure in the film and dealt with that discomfort through a process of disavowal, thus raising the issue of the role of the female body in classical cinema as producing both meaning and pleasure for an audience. *Pumping Iron II*, she argues, "transcends this inscription of the female body to interrogate that body and its limits" (Kuhn, 1988, p. 16). In the end, the film never resolves the question of what, precisely, is a woman's body.

Laurie Schulze's (1990) brilliant "reading" of women's bodybuilding shows that the female bodybuilder continues to cause considerable ideological strain. In her words,

> A female body displaying "extreme" muscle mass, separation and definition, yet oiled up, clad in a bikini, marked with conventionally "feminine"-styled hair and carefully applied cosmetics juxtaposes heterogeneous elements in a way that frustrates ideological unity and confounds common sense. (p. 68)

It is because of this dissonance that people often find women bodybuilders "grotesque" or "freakish" assuming that they wish to look like men, or, worse, actually wish to be men. In fact, the dominant culture often links female bodybuilding with lesbianism, which is one explanation for the subculture's vigorous attempts to "anchor female bodybuilders to heterosexuality" (Schulze, 1990, p. 73). She concludes her discussion by suggesting that there is still much work to do on the issues posed by female bodybuilding. It is, she argues, "ideologically messy enough, open and ambiguous enough, polysemic [having many meanings] enough to be relevant to people with very dissimilar social allegiances" (p. 78). I agree, but I admit to being pleasantly surprised when I discovered the quantity and quality of the existing cultural work on women's bodybuilding.[14] It is a good example of what is possible around the body in other areas of women's sport and leisure.

Some Thoughts on Future Research

In chapter 3 I pointed out that the reconstruction of women's sporting and leisure experiences is a vastly underresearched area. Sexuality, female physicality, and the "long-standing hegemonic control that men have claimed over women's bodies" are central to the history of women's sport (Vertinsky, 1994, p. 23). Primarily through the work of feminist sport historians, we now know much more about the dominating influence of the medical establishment (especially in Victorian times), the media, and modern psychology upon women's bodies and sporting lives. Also, a new genre of "body history" has become prominent in the last decade fostered in part by the developing histories of women, minority groups, and "ordinary" people, but also by recent developments in the history of medicine and health. Yet as Roberta Park (1994) concludes in her detailed review of historical work on health, fitness, exercise, and the body over the past decade, the history of women's health and exercise in relation to the body remains largely unexplored. Therefore, among our first priorities is to get on with the necessary and important historical work.[15]

Just as it is essential to understand the historical construction of women's bodily oppression—their struggle to express bodily competence, force, and power—so too is it necessary to explore women's current struggles around the subordination of their physicality. What we need are concrete, material analyses of diverse women's "body" experience in sport. For example, I have long been impressed with the work of Frigga Haug and the West German *Frauenformen* collective.[16] In the work of the collective and in their writings, the female body is the axis around which sexuality is organized in childhood and in everyday practices whereby girls learn to be women. The project itself is a process in which members of the collective write down memories of past events that focus on a specific physical area (hair, legs, stomach, etc.). These memories are written in light of a collective critique in order to reconstruct the processes through which the female body becomes sexualized, controlled, and oppressed. Understanding these processes is the basis to all further feminist practice.

I believe we could use the same collective technique to discover and reconstruct the processes whereby female bodies become moving, active, and physical, as well as the processes through which so many women are denied this power. Although done individually and not in a collective, the memory work of Finnish researcher Ulla Kosonen (1993a) on the "body of a running girl" is what I have in mind. Growing up in the 1960s, she recounts her story of the clumsy girl, big for her age and ridiculed because of it, who found solace and escape in running. In an accompanying essay, Kosonen (1993b) argues for the importance and validity of individual memory work, suggesting that it is "the ultimate example of subject and object collapsing into each other in research" (p. 51). Similar work, but done in a collective setting, linked to feminist body theory and ultimately to practice would be very powerful.

We also need more studies in which women athletes are asked to reflect upon the significance of the body and physicality to their experience of sport. For example, Genevieve Rail (1990, 1992), in her phenomenological study of physical contact in women's basketball, shows how women athletes use the physicality of their game, and the emotionality that surrounds it, as "lived experiences" through which they learn about (and question) their self-identities.

In another study, Nancy Theberge (1995) argues that the real cultural significance of sport lies in its power to represent and embody beliefs about gender, physicality, and sexual difference. She uses ice hockey, which in Canada enjoys status as a "flag carrier of masculinity," to illustrate the contested terrain of gender, in this case struggles over the body and physicality. At the competitive level, men's and women's hockey are substantially the same, except the rules of women's hockey prohibit *intentional* body checking; in other words, one plays the puck, not the body. Nevertheless, there is still considerable body contact in the women's game as players constantly outmanoeuvre and outmuscle each other, often colliding against the boards. What is interesting here, as Theberge documents, is that the players themselves are ambivalent as to whether or not intentional body checking should be a part of the women's game. Some argue that this very physicality is the essence of the game; otherwise it is not "real" hockey. Others note that the elimination of checking has reduced the risk of serious injury and thus made the game attractive to a greater number of players. However, as Theberge suggests, the removal of body checking produces an alternative form of the game that reinforces the status of women's hockey as "other" and confirms the inferiority of women's sport. Finally, Sheila Scraton's (1992) studies of the social construction of girls' physicality in British physical education curricula, programs, and classes are extremely valuable in helping us understand the potential role (as yet unrealized) of school physical education in challenging myths concerning female bodies, strength, and physicality.

Kevin Young and Philip White (1995) have examined women's subjective experiences and meanings attached to participation in contact, high-injury, and otherwise physically dangerous sports like rugby, basketball, downhill skiing, and football. What is interesting about their study (based, however, on only 12 women) when compared to a similar study with male athletes is the remarkable gender similarities in the attitudes to physical danger, aggression, and injury. Female athletes were as willing as men to expose themselves to physical risk; both groups unquestionably accepted the "no pain, no gain" philosophy of male-defined sport; and both were relatively unreflexive about the meaning and significance of violent, excessive, and health-compromising sport. This sort of research, although unsettling, is needed because it helps us understand women's complicity in the ways that the body is often exploited and abused through sport. As sport psychologist Mary Duquin (1994b) comments in her stinging critique of abusive sport systems, "this kind of athlete socialization not only produces weak and passive political subjects but undermines athlete unity on political issues relevant to the general health and welfare of athletes" (p. 275).

I elaborate on the need to politicize both women's sport and women in sport in chapter 6, but in the next chapter, I expand on some of the research ideas suggested here through a more careful analysis of what, precisely, constitutes feminist research.

Notes

1. For recent calls within the sociology of sport to pay much more attention to the body, see Andrews (1993), Gruneau (1993), John Hargreaves (1986, 1987), Harvey and Sparks (1991), Loy, Andrews and Rinehart (1993), Maguire (1993), Shilling (1993), and Theberge (1991).

2. Elizabeth Grosz (1994, pp. 15-19) argues for three categories or positions within feminist theory around conceptions of the body. First is *egalitarian feminism* where the specificities of the female body—menstruation, pregnancy, maternity, lactation, etc.—are on the one hand regarded as a limitation to women's access to rights and privileges, and on the other as a unique means of access to knowledge and ways of living. Thus, biology itself requires modification and transformation. Most liberal, conservative, and humanist feminists such as Simone de Beauvoir, Shulamith Firestone, and Mary Wollstonecraft subscribe to this position. The second category is *social constructionism*. The majority of feminist thinkers today are social constructionists, who have a more positive attitude toward the body than the first group, arguing that it is not biology per se but the ways in which the social system organizes and gives meaning to biology that is oppressive to women. The project of this group has been to minimize biological differences and to provide them with different cultural meanings and values. The last position she labels as *sexual difference*. This category is represented by theorists like Luce Irigary, Hélène Cixous, Gayatri Spivak, Jane Gallop, Moira Gatens, Vicki Kirby, Judith Butler, Naomi Schor, and Monique Wittig. Unlike the other two groups, they do not view the body as an ahistorical, biologically given, acultural object; they are concerned with the body as it is represented and used in specific ways in particular cultures, in other words, the "lived" body. This group is also wary of the sex/gender distinction arguing against sex as an essentialist category and gender as a constructionist category; they seek to undermine this very dichotomy along with the mind/body dualism.

3. For historical accounts, see Cahn (1990, 1994) and Theberge (1989) in the United States, Fletcher (1984) in Britain, and Lenskyj (1983, 1986) in Canada.

4. A more general definition of "dualisms" is the belief that there are two mutually exclusive types of "thing," physical and mental, body and mind, that compose the universe in general and subjectivity in particular (Grosz, 1994, p. vii).

5. According to Rosenau (1992), there is considerable overlap between postmodernism and poststructuralism and little effort has been made to distinguish them. Poststructuralists, she suggests, emphasize method and epistemological matters by concentrating on deconstruction, language,

discourse, meaning, and symbols, whereas postmodernists are more oriented toward cultural critique and cast a broader net (p. 3). Postmodernism and poststructuralism both pose a challenge to the underlying assumptions of mainstream social science (and other disciplines) by rejecting epistemological assumptions, refuting methodological conventions, resisting knowledge claims, obscuring all versions of truth, and dismissing policy recommendations. She also suggests that how one writes these terms—with or without a hyphen—denotes whether one is a sympathizer (no hyphen) or a critic (hyphen). Personally, I think it is possible to be *both* a sympathizer and critic of postmodernist theorizing.

6. For example, see Diamond and Quinby (1988), McNay (1992), Ramazanoglu (1993), and Sawicki (1991).

7. In what follows, I discuss only the first two of these waves primarily because I have found examples to illustrate them within feminist sport studies. The leading postmodernist feminist theorist of the third wave is Judith Butler (1990, 1993), but I could find no application of her work to sport and leisure, nor was I prepared to engage in such an application myself. Also, Butler proposes that gender is both discursively and materially constructed through repetitive "performances" of "words, acts, gestures and desire," and she calls for a notion of sexuality as a "site of contestation and subversion" (see Deveaux, 1994, p. 237-242). I am not comfortable, nor sufficiently familiar, with these ideas to assess their appropriative value, and I am wary of their usefulness in laying out an appropriate feminist political practice.

8. Internet surfers can now find considerable information about women's bodybuilding via The Female Bodybuilder Home Page, which contains information on magazines, books, organizations, photos, videos, and contest placings in addition to links to separate home pages of several "standout" female bodybuilders and photos of these women.

9. It is important to distinguish bodybuilding from weightlifting activities engaged in by people who use gyms and health clubs for keeping fit or body toning. Bodybuilders deliberately cultivate an increase in mass and strength of the skeletal muscles by means of lifting and pushing weight (Mansfield & McGinn, 1993).

10. See, for example, Duff and Hong (1984), Franck (1984), Freeman (1988), and Pugh (1993).

11. Bolin (1992b) makes the point that Bev Francis is also an excellent case‧ study in the "construction of beauty." Mansfield and McGinn (1993) suggest that "it would be difficult to find a more powerful commentary on the way in which the woman bodybuilder constructs her body to fulfill the twin constraints of aesthetic and safe femininity than the career of Bev Francis, and the changes she has made to her body in order to become a successful bodybuilder" (p. 63).

12. In a fascinating essay on the growing "transgender community," Bolin (1994) uses women's bodybuilding to show how members of that com-

munity have been positively influenced by changes and challenges to embodiments of femininity. The "new muscular soma" of women, as expressed, for example, in women bodybuilders and highly athletic women, has benefited male cross-dressers and male-to-female transsexuals allowing them (and their bodies) to be more easily accepted in society, indeed to "pass" more successfully as women.

13. There are other feminist analyses and critiques of the *Pumping Iron II: The Women* film, such as Holmlund (1989) and Balsamo (1994), both of which deal, among other issues, with how race is perceived and constructed in the film. The winner of the contest was Carla Dunlap who at the time was one of the few black professional women bodybuilders. Their analyses highlight the ways in which the natural female body is culturally reconstructed, via bodybuilding, according to the dominant codes of femininity and racial identity.

14. A new book of feminist critique on bodybuilding is due out in 1996— Pamela Moore (Ed.), *The Built Body Anthology*, New York: Rutgers University Press.

15. The history of women's sport in 20th-century North America, for example, is one of ongoing tension between women's separate evolution of sporting practices and forms, and at the same time, their contested appropriation of similar masculine cultural forms. This history, in my view, is best traced through the various discourses of the female sporting body: primarily the medical, the legal, the health/beauty, the organizational, the media, the education/physical education, the sport science, and the feminist. My current, ongoing research is about how these particular discourses evolved and how in turn they have affected the female sporting body in 20th-century Canada (see M.A. Hall, in press). For other new and exciting historical work on sporting bodies, see the *Sport Science Review*, **4**(1), 1995 edited by sport historian Gertrud Pfister.

16. Frigga Haug is a well-known feminist and Marxist critic in Germany. Some of her work is available in English in *Female Sexualization: A Collective Work of Memory* (1983), which details the sexualization of women's bodies through collective memory work. A second, more recent volume is *Beyond Female Masochism: Memory-work and Politics* (1992) which is a series of essays exploring the links between the micropolitics of daily life and the evolving structures of capitalism.

The "Doing" of Feminist Research

5

I remember many years ago reading somewhere that feminism was not about who goes through the door first, but about a way of being in the world and how we know what we know. I have since put fancy labels on the latter, namely, *ontology*, the philosophical study of the nature of being or reality, and *epistemology*, the study of the origin, nature, methods, and limits of knowledge. At the time, however, I had no idea that this is where my studies in feminism would eventually lead.

I admited in the first chapter that I unwittingly began my research career as a positivist, becoming very proficient in the "science" of social research—operationalizing concepts, developing indicators, collecting data, testing theory, and so on. In fact, I still teach this material, although it is very humbling to drag out my now 20-year-old dissertation to illustrate the finer points of causal model building. I do this in the context of a graduate-level course that exposes students to what it means to do quantitative, qualitative, and, more important, "critical" inquiry.

Feminism has had the most impact on how I now view (and do) social inquiry. I wrote about this in a 1985 article entitled "Knowledge and Gender: Epistemological Questions in the Social Analysis of

Sport.'' My purpose was to show the importance of the feminist challenge to the origin, nature, methods, and limits of knowledge that have shaped our understanding of social life, and to examine the implications for the social analysis of sport. The more central question explored in the essay was whether there could be a distinctive feminist epistemology, and if there was, what would this mean for our social inquiry into women's sport. I outlined the major assumptions that I felt at the time identified a distinctly feminist epistemology: (a) the necessity of a standpoint and of the standpoint of women in particular; (b) the challenge to objectivism and the rejection of positivism; (c) the rejection of a hierarchy of dualisms; and (d) the recognition of a transformative potential in a feminist theory of knowledge. At the same time, I had little to say about the specific methodological implications that stem from the feminist challenge to traditional social inquiry, and the actual doing of feminist research.

A decade later, I can now call on a vastly expanded literature that addresses the debate over feminist research principles and expounds the complex connections between feminist epistemologies, methodologies, and research methods.[1] These debates and relationships are the focus of this chapter, as well as the topic of a women's studies course I taught for several years. The chapter begins with an examination of the meaning and relationship between epistemology, methodology, and method by addressing the question: Do feminists need epistemology? I then discuss the fundamental question of what it means to do feminist research. In the last two sections I focus on how to make our research more relevant to the everyday world of women's sport and discuss the relationship between an epistemological stance and the research one conducts, feminist research as praxis, and the implications for policy-oriented research in the area of gender equity.

Do Feminists Need Epistemology?

Most students are familiar with the *methods* of social inquiry. These are the techniques for gathering evidence such as surveys, interviews, field work, ethnography, and the like. *Methodology*, on the other hand, is a perspective or broad theoretical framework about how research should proceed, which in social research often comes down to the quantitative as opposed to the qualitative. Surveys, experiments, secondary analyses, structured observations, and numerical content analyses fit most logically into the quantitative framework, whereas participant observation, unstructured and in-depth interviewing, life histories, case studies, action research, and other methods define qualitative methodology. However, as I discuss presently, the quantitative/qualitative methodological division is not as clear-cut as it might seem.

Epistemology points to presuppositions about the nature of knowledge, and of scientific inquiry, that inform research. It addresses central questions like who can be a "knower," what can be known, what constitutes and validates knowledge, and what is the relationship between knowing and being (Stanley & Wise, 1990). The conception of knowledge that has dominated Western intellectual traditions at least since the 17th century is known as Enlightenment epistemology, or foundationalism.[2] Two dominant epistemological positions emerge from foundationalism. Positivism (sometimes referred to as empiricism or objectivism) claims that epistemologically the social sciences are no different from the natural sciences and that they should, as a consequence, mimic the methods of the natural sciences. In opposition to positivism is interpretationalism (sometimes referred to as the phenomenological), which accepts that there are similarities between the social and natural sciences but insists that they require different methodologies.[3] It sees the goal of social science as understanding, not explanation. It should come as no surprise that feminist social researchers have been more willing to embrace the epistemological stance of interpretationalism, and hence qualitative rather than quantitative methods. But the issue is not nearly this simple.

The literature in this area focuses on some fundamental, yet difficult questions. Is epistemology the foundation of method and methodology, and do epistemological issues underpin the so-called division between quantitative and qualitative methodologies? Do researchers chose only those methods that are consistent with their epistemological stance? Is there a unique feminist epistemology (or perhaps epistemologies), and if so, does it support specific "feminist methods"? Finally, what is the relationship between feminist epistemology and ontology?

The simplest answer to these questions, and others, is that they are dilemmas that have absolutely no solutions (Reinharz, 1992). There are now a myriad of ongoing discussions on these issues not only between feminist and nonfeminist (often antifeminist) scholars, but also among feminist researchers. What I do know is that as a feminist researcher it is important to have at least a broad understanding of these debates and issues. Thinking and reading about them, and certainly trying to teach them, has made me more reflexive and critical of my own research processes.

It is also important to recognize that the debates about feminist scholarship and research take place on different levels. For instance, feminist philosophers have entered the fray, along with postmodernists and poststructuralists, by challenging Enlightenment epistemology itself.[4] This antifoundationalism rejects all attempts to find an absolute grounding for knowledge; rejects the rationalist model as the only model of knowledge; asserts that there is not one but many models for knowledge, and hence truths; and rejects the dichotomies upon which Enlightenment epistemology rests (subject/object, reason/emotion, nature/culture, etc.). Feminists have contributed to these debates by identifying Enlightenment rationalism as a distinctly male mode of thought by showing that its dualisms are rooted in the male/female dichotomy that is central to patriarchal thought and society (Hekman, 1987).

Feminist philosophers have also been intent on addressing the question of what theory of knowledge, what epistemology (or epistemologies) can provide a "justifiable guide to practical decisions that have effects on women's lives" (Harding, 1990, p. 89). Women, of course, are not a homogeneous social group. We vary across cultures, and we vary due to structures of domination in our own societies such as age, race, class, disability, and sexual orientation. Therefore, according to Harding, we need theories of knowledge that not only recognize these differences, but also "motivate and enable us to work against exploitative relations between women" (1990, p. 90). I also agree with her when she says,

> Feminist sciences and epistemologies should help to bring to consciousness less mystified understandings of women's and men's situations so that these understandings can energize and direct women and men to struggle on behalf of eliminating the subordination of women in all its race, class, and cultural forms. (p. 90)

Harding has done valuable synthesis work in identifying appropriate "justificatory strategies" or epistemologies.[5] In her view, there are three such epistemologies—feminist empiricism, feminist standpoint theory, and feminist postmodernism—although all of them are ongoing and incomplete projects.

Feminist empiricism challenges how the scientific method has been practised, but it neglects to question the norms of science itself and concludes that sexism and androcentrism in scientific inquiry are entirely the consequence of poorly conducted research. For example, Canadian sociologist Margrit Eichler, in her useful book on nonsexist research methods, identifies androcentricity, overgeneralization, overspecification, gender insensitivity, double standards, sex appropriateness, familism, and sexual dichotomism as the components of sexism in research (Eichler, 1986). Nevertheless, feminist empiricism has contributed significantly to exposing the androcentric bias in nearly every academic discipline (Kramarae & Spender, 1992) and has produced a "knowledge explosion" about women's lives and realities. In chapter 2, I pointed out the value of distributive research, a form of empiricism that examines the distribution of resources and focuses on inequalities. This approach continues to produce useful knowledge about women's position in the sports world and is sometimes used as a starting point for further analysis and action.

Feminist standpoint theory[6] begins with the premise that "experiences arising from the activities assigned to women, understood through feminist theory, provide a starting point for developing potentially more complete and less distorted knowledge claims than do men's experiences" (Harding, 1990, p. 95). For example, Canadian sociologist Dorothy Smith (1979, 1987) argues that women's actual experiences of their own activities are often incomprehensible and inexpressible within the distorted abstractions of men's conceptual schemes.

Here is an illustration of what she means. As every woman who is a full-time housewife and/or mother can tell us, there is little distinction between being at work and not being at work in the home. Once it is recognized that housework and child care are work, and that being responsible for the lives of other human beings means that one is always at work in some sense, then distinctions between work and nonwork are simply not appropriate. Yet we have innumerable accounts that make use of the work-leisure dichotomy, and sociologists do research on the "leisure" of housewives and mothers. "If we started with housework as the basis," argues Dorothy Smith (1979), "the categories of 'work' and 'leisure' would never emerge" (p. 154). In fact, she points out that if we were to use housework as our basic framework, it would be difficult to imagine how to make work and leisure observable. What feminist standpoint theory exposes is that women are alienated from their own experience by the use of the dominant, *male*stream conceptual schemes (Harding, 1990).

I mentioned earlier that some feminists have joined the anti-Enlightenment camp, and along with postmodernists and poststructuralists, are challenging Enlightenment epistemology, which means confronting the assumptions upon which feminist empiricism and the feminist standpoint are based. They argue that postmodernism is a natural ally of feminism because there are many points of overlap (Nicholson, 1990). For instance, both are critical of the alleged neutrality and political power of academe and of knowledge claims. Both reject theory that generalizes from the experiences of Western, white, middle-class, heterosexual men and women. Both challenge global, all-encompassing world views, be they political, religious, or social (Rosenau, 1992). Both question rigid disciplinary boundaries within academe. And, as I have already discussed, most feminists are in agreement with postmodernists in the rejection of the positivist, empiricist, rational-logic model of modern science. Yet as British sociologists Liz Stanley and Sue Wise (1993) remind us, there is nothing really original in these epistemological claims in that they have appeared before in critiques of positivism in their own earlier work and in the work of other feminists influenced by "interactionism" (their term for reflexive sociologies such as phenomenology, ethnomethodology, and symbolic interactionism).

Nearly all scholars, however, would argue that we are now in a postpositivist period in the human sciences, one marked by methodological and epistemological ferment (Lather, 1991). As a result there is a spectrum of feminist epistemological positions. These differing stances argue for sometimes conflicting ideas about who knows what, about whom, and how this knowledge is legitimized. Finally, there can be no "right" or "correct" feminist epistemology, and there can be no hegemony of one form of feminism over all others.

More methodologically oriented feminist researchers have chided feminist philosophers, whose debates tend to be somewhat esoteric, because their research remains at the abstract level of epistemology. "There is a problem," observes Mary Maynard (1994), "in linking some of the arguments made at the epistemological level with what happens, or should happen, in terms of research practice and the use of particular research techniques'' (p. 21). Similarly, Liz Stanley and Sue Wise (1990, 1993) ask how epistemology can be put into practice methodologically and how it relates to the practical use of different research techniques. How, they ask, should a substantive feminist research process, which is concerned with actual living, breathing, thinking, theorising people, proceed at the level of methodology and translate into method? I turn to these issues in the next section.

What Is Feminist Research?

Epistemologically, we must accept that there are women's *ways* of knowing. Therefore, it follows that feminist research practices reflect this plurality and that there can be no one feminist method. Feminism, asserts Shulamit Reinharz (1992), supplies the theoretical perspective; and the disciplines furnish the method. The feminist researcher exists at the intersection of the two with one foot in the discipline, the academy, or the organisation funding the research, and the other in the world of feminist scholarship. There is no single ''feminist way'' to do research; in fact, there is a great deal of individual creativity and variety. There is also an affinity between feminist research and cross-disciplinary work, which in some institutions has found a home in women's studies. I know personally that doing feminist research has forced me to go outside my area of study, and it has been stimulating to explore a variety of work in other disciplines.

What then distinguishes feminist research practice from traditional social research practice?[7] Although there is no real consensus among feminist researchers as to the answer, I think it is possible to lay out several defining characteristics. The first, which I have already mentioned, is that feminist research is derived from a theoretical perspective that acknowledges the pervasive influence of gender divisions on social life. Feminist research is guided by feminist theory because other theoretical traditions ignore or downplay the interaction of gender and power. This in itself, however, is not that helpful because, as I have continually stressed, there are now many theoretical positions taken up by those who claim feminism as a label. Also, as Maynard (1994) points out, it is not entirely clear what focusing on gender means in terms of the subjects of our research. Should our focus be entirely on women, or also on men and relations between women and men? I argue throughout this book for a ''relational'' approach to gender (and age, class, race, ethnicity, disability, and sexuality) that recognizes unequal relationships between dominant and subordinate groups and acknowledges that sport plays a role in the construction of those relationships and their persistence over time. Therefore, feminist research from this position could focus either solely on women, on men (providing this is helpful to women), or on the relations between them.

What is also not clear is the relationship of gender to other forms of oppression and how to conduct research that takes this into account. In chapter 3, in the section on differences among women, I pointed to the obvious white bias of our scholarship within feminist sport studies and to the neglect of critical relational analyses of the intersections of gender, race, class, and other classifications upon which oppression is based. I also argue that as researchers we regularly universalize "women's experiences in sport" as if there was some "generic" sporting woman when, in fact, all women do not experience sport in the same way, if indeed they experience it at all.[8] One way out is to address, through appropriate research, the silences of our previous empirical work. However, as Maynard (1994) cautions,

> To imply that matters of class are significant to the experience of the working class alone, that "race" is important for only some ethnic groups (for to be white is also to have ethnicity), or that sexuality is relevant only to lesbians and gays is to miss the point. For these things structure *all* our lives, no matter how invisible they might be in experiential terms, and we are not excused from confronting them because we are not members of a particular oppressed group. (p. 24)

A second way in which the feminist research process has become refined is through modifications to existing research techniques or methods (Maynard, 1994). In her splendid compilation of feminist methods in social research, Reinharz (1992) details the usual social research methods (e.g., interview, ethnography, survey, experimental, oral history, cross-cultural, content analysis, case study, action research) and provides countless examples of how feminists have used these methods for their own ends. For example, feminists have made extensive use of interviewing and ethnography in their research, but at the same time, they have been critical of the ways in which much sociological research involves hierarchical power relationships between the researcher and the researched (Maynard, 1994). Feminist researchers working with people attempt to develop nonexploitative relations with those involved in their research projects by promoting relations of respect, shared information, openness, and clarity of communication (Reinharz, 1992). Utilizing the researcher's personal experience is often considered a modification in feminist research. This requires some courage to violate the norms of so-called dispassionate research (using "I" for example) and to work out the resulting tension between subjectivity and objectivity. I provided an example of this sort of experiential research in chapter 4 in the discussion of individual and collective "memory work" around women's body experiences in sport and physical activity.

A third way in which feminist research is distinctive is in its "insistence on its political nature and potential to bring about change in women's lives" (Maynard, 1994, p. 16). Again, this raises some important and often divisive issues. For example, are research studies that cannot be linked to "transformational politics" therefore not feminist? It should be obvious that not all feminist research can or should produce knowledge that will transform patriarchy, even if such a goal were possible. The researcher is often not in control of any changes, certainly not at the systemic level, that her research may suggest.

Feminists have been enthusiastic promoters of change-oriented research, which includes action research, participatory/collaborative research, prevalence and needs assessment, evaluation research, and demystification (Reinharz, 1992). Change-oriented research implies that women can be empowered to change their situations through either doing their own research or through participation in a research project.[9] However, as Maynard (1994) points out, not all outcomes may be positive; and although women may have their consciousness raised, there may be no opportunities for them to take action. But she also stresses that even if the research has little impact on the individuals, it may contribute positively to broader changes in the behaviour of agencies, or to legislation and policy.

In sum, feminist social research practice is tremendously varied, is not without contradiction and controversy, and is in the process of development. I want now to return to some of the epistemological and methodological issues I raised earlier and in doing so make clear my own position and suggestions for a feminist research practice in sport.

Feminist Research as Praxis

In *Getting Smart: Feminist Research and Pedagogy With/In the Postmodern*, United States educator Patti Lather (1991) outlines what she calls the paradigms of postpositivist inquiry. Their basis lies in what German philosopher and social critic Jürgen Habermas defined as "the categories of human interest" that underscore all knowledge claims, namely, prediction, understanding, emancipation, and a fourth added by Lather, deconstruction. Each of these paradigms offers "a different approach to generating and legitimating knowledge; each is a contender for allegiance" (p. 7). Under the *prediction* paradigm is positivism; although certainly not dead, it no longer has the same grip on theory and practice in the human sciences as it once did. Several methodological stances fall within the *understanding* paradigm (what Harding labels "interpretationalism") and they go by a variety of names: interpretive, naturalistic, phenomenological, hermeneutic, and symbolic interaction. The *emancipation* paradigm, a direct challenge to both prediction and understanding, also encompasses a variety of theoretical and methodological stances such as neo-Marxist, critical theory, praxis-oriented, participatory, and here Lather also includes feminist. Finally, she places both postmodernism and poststructuralism under the *deconstruction* paradigm defined as "to keep things in process, to disrupt, to keep the system in play, to set up procedures to continuously demystify the realities we create, to fight the tendency for our categories to congeal" (Lather, 1991, p. 13).

Lather's typology is a useful way to conceptualize the dramatic and exciting shifts in the paradigms of social inquiry within the social sciences that have occurred over a relatively short period of time, specifically the last 30 to 40 years. These include the "failure" of positivism, although it still has a vigorous hold on psychology; the realization that merely understanding the world is insufficient to bring about social change; the increasing acceptance of an overtly value-based and openly ideological critical social science; and the unsettling influence of poststructuralism and postmodernism, which profoundly challenge the politics of emancipation.

As I discussed earlier in the section on epistemology, the discourses of feminism can be found within each of these four paradigms, although positivism is strongly rejected even by feminist psychologists. Empiricism, however, or the search for knowledge through observation and experiment, is certainly not dismissed. Feminist psychologists in particular continue to utilize experiments for feminist goals (e.g., the gendered power dynamics of nonverbal behaviour and interaction), while at the same time criticizing the many inherent flaws and sexism in traditional experimental research (Reinharz, 1992). Many feminist sociologists have felt comfortable with the understanding paradigm and have promoted the use of a variety of methodologies within the interpretive framework (see, for example, Levesque-Lopman, 1988, on phenomenology; Deegan & Hill, 1987, on symbolic interaction). A massive body of scholarship has been produced by feminists who engage the major theoretical positions that ground critical and emancipatory social inquiry, namely, critical theory, Marxism, and hegemony theory. Their research projects are politically guided and have produced "less partial and distorted results of research than those supposedly guided by the goal of value-neutrality" (Harding, 1993, p. 49). Emancipatory research has been *for* women in the sense that it provides more "valid" answers to questions that arise from women's lives, *and* according to Harding, "about the rest of nature and social relations" (p. 50). Finally, over the past decade there has been a significant "turn to culture" in feminism, and this marked interest in analyzing processes of symbolization and representation rather than in models of social structure indicates a disciplinary shift from the social sciences to the arts, humanities, and philosophy (Barrett, 1990, 1992). In part, this explains the increasing interest in deconstruction, postmodernism, and poststructuralism by many feminists in all disciplinary areas.

Where does all this leave us? My own intellectual journey, although by no means at the last signpost, has been to travel from positivism, with some dabbling along the way in the understanding paradigm, to having both feet firmly planted in critical and emancipatory social research. My steps are noticeably slower these days as I try to make sense of the challenges posed by postmodernism and to wade through the virtual explosion of deconstructionist

scholarship descending on the path. However, I am heartened by the advice
of two "friends" (we have never met) whose work I have followed for years,
that of British sociologists Liz Stanley and Sue Wise. *Breaking Out Again*
(1993) is a reprint of their earlier *Breaking Out*, published in 1983, but it
also includes an insightful reading of the original text and an additional essay
arguing that the issues and questions dealt with originally continue to be at
the centre of contemporary feminist theory a decade later. They caution,
however, that recent debates within feminist social theory are old feminist
wine in new deconstructionist bottles, expressed in a more mystificatory and
abstract way. Although they recognize that academic feminism is much more
professionalized than it was a decade ago, they criticize its specialist language
and accompanying "language games," reminding us that *feminist praxis*,
rather than a preoccupation with the text, is the proper feminist political
engagement within academic life. Others are even more critical of academic
feminism, lamenting that the relationship of feminist research to the struggle
for women's liberation has ceased to be a central concern (Kelly, Burton, &
Regan, 1994).

What is meant here by praxis? It is a recognition of the continuing and
shared feminist commitment to a political position in which "knowledge"
is not simply defined as "what knowledge" but also as "knowledge for,"
and in this case *for* women. As Liz Stanley (1990) states so clearly,

> Feminism outside the academic mode has insisted on the crucial need
> for useful knowledge, theory and research as practice, on committed
> understanding as a form of praxis ("understand the world and then
> change it"), and also on an unalienated knowledge. (p. 12)

Praxis, therefore, acknowledges that what goes on in academe, at least as
far as feminism is concerned, should be directed at producing the kind of useful
knowledge wanted and needed by those outside academe who are working for
social change. The issue then is how to connect theory and research to the real
world. In an interesting essay about recognizing one's theories as "useless ivory-
tower exercises," sport sociologist Michael Messner (1992b, p. 137) argues that
the key question is not "should our research be engaged with the real world,"
but rather, "whose interests should our research serve?" The answer for feminists
is quite simple—women.

In the world of sport feminism, unfortunately, there is a noticeable gap
between our theory/research and our practice. There are literally millions
of participants, athletes, coaches, administrators, officials, educators, and
volunteers all working toward the betterment of women's sport and gender
equity for whom this theorizing and research is completely foreign. I have
argued that those working in academe, whose focus is research and scholarship, should be working hand in hand with those on the "front line"—be
they participants, competitors, teachers, coaches, professional and volunteer
leaders, policy makers, or activists. There should, in my view, be more

concern among feminist sport researchers over the unification of theory and practice, the personal and the political: in sum, what I have defined here as praxis.

Venturing Onto the Front Line: Feminist Researchers and Praxis-Oriented Research

Sport itself has been stubbornly resistant to feminism, and it remains a highly conservative institution. Although there has been some improvement in recent years, attempts to institute gender equity in the sports world have been by and large unsuccessful. As I show in more detail in the next chapter, feminist activism around sport has been almost entirely "liberal" in philosophy and strategy. The problem with most liberal approaches is that they call for solutions focusing on individuals rather than on issues of systemic power and privilege. For example, the "role model" approach, in which successful female athletes are used to provide positive examples for other girls and women to follow, does little to address the various forms of systemic discrimination and harassment that make it impossible for many girls and women to emulate those role models (Lenskyj, 1994). Gender equity programs (e.g., removal of discriminatory hiring policies, affirmative action) aimed at increasing the numbers of women in sport leadership positions are obviously helpful, but when these same women are isolated, receive little support, and have limited networking opportunities, then social change initiatives remain at the individual rather than at the collective level. Also, if women and minorities experience an unwelcome or unsafe environment caused by the "chilly climate," then it is not sufficient to simply "open the door" if the resulting "chilly blast" forces them out again (Lenskyj, 1994, p. 30). The general problem, and the primary reason why gender equity programs in sport have not been as successful as we would hope, is that women's experience, behaviour, personality, or values in sport are seen as "deficient," and women are asked time and time again to change and fit into male-defined, male-dominated systems. Again, Helen Lenskyj is worth quoting here:

> This "female deficit" model upholds traditional male values and attitudes in sport as the ideal. Female perspectives are judged by the male standard and found lacking, and women are then blamed for having the "wrong" attitude. (p. 7)

Given this background, the purpose of this section is to explore the notion of gender-related, praxis-oriented (some prefer the term "policy-oriented") research within the sport setting. What is it like, from the researcher's perspective, to actually do this kind of research? What problems are encountered? What tensions and conflicts do policy-oriented researchers face when their research is funded by the organisations that either directly or indirectly are the focus of this research? It is important not to minimize the problems here, and it is also important to understand just how difficult it is to engage in any form of feminist research with sport-related organisations and funding bodies. From a research perspective, however, it is critical that sport researchers write about and publish their experiences, both good and bad, about the process of doing feminist research in the sports world so that we all can learn and benefit from these experiences. Here are three examples, the first of which describes some of my own encounters in this area.

Several years ago two colleagues and I were involved in a large-scale study concerning the gender structure of Canadian national sport organisations (M.A. Hall, Cullen, & Slack, 1989, 1990). The project was initiated by Sport Canada, the federal government agency responsible for the administration and funding of amateur sport in Canada, which asked us to examine why the status of women, in terms of participation and leadership opportunities, was changing in some national sport organisations (NSOs) but not in others. Each NSO has a volunteer structure that often includes a board of directors, an executive committee, provincial representatives, and specialized committees. Overall, women comprise approximately 25 percent of this volunteer structure, although there is considerable variance among the NSOs. Our research questions focused on the ways in which an NSO's environment, structure, culture, and resource allocations affect the opportunities for females within that organisation. The project proceeded in two phases. The first was a case study of five sports selected by Sport Canada to provide a range of organisations, from those that had demonstrated their receptivity to improving the status of women (e.g., cycling) to those that remained firm in their belief that there simply was no gender equity problem (e.g., swimming). In this phase of the project, we relied primarily on interviews (approximately 70) with key people, especially women, whom we identified from the volunteer and professional structure of each organisation. The second phase of the project expanded the study to an additional seven sports in order to provide a broader range of organisations in terms of their environment, structure, culture, resource allocations, and receptivity to improving the status of women. Phase two was a more systematic investigation (utilizing an extensive questionnaire) in which we surveyed the key volunteers (both men and women)— primarily members of executive committees and boards of directors, provincial representatives, and members of national-level committees— in all twelve sports.

What we found was that men and women perceive the problem of female underrepresentation in their organisations in very different ways. Only about one third of the men (as opposed to two thirds of the women) admitted that systemic discrimination was the problem, and they placed it low on their list of possible reasons. Although the relative importance of factors such as family constraints, success of male networks, being aware of available positions, weakness of female networks, and lack of training opportunities was approximately the same for both sexes, many more women than men believed these factors to be significant. As one male respondent put it,

> If one is willing to take risks, grab opportunities, and make the sacrifices required (just as *all* previous successful people who started near the bottom have) then gender is *virtually a non-issue* in terms of climbing the *chosen* ladder of success. (emphasis in the original) (Hall et al., 1990, p. 27)

What this particular individual identified was the considerable difficulty most of our respondents (65 percent were male) had in accepting that there was a problem in the first place. Most firmly believed either that women were represented in their organisation in proportion to their numbers as participants (although in none of the twelve sports we studied was this actually the case), or that their sport was wide open to anyone of either sex providing they were qualified and willing to work. Although the women saw the problem differently, gender issues were mostly *non-issues* for the vast majority of individuals, both male and female, in these organisations. Thus, even though the women in our study saw many problems that were organisationally based (e.g., success of male networks), they, along with men, were generally opposed to the idea of a gender equity policy or program in their organisation on the grounds that equal opportunity already existed. These seemingly paradoxical perceptions are understandable if women believe they have overcome barriers because of luck or having links with the "right" people, or, as one woman put it, "I feel our sport needs and wants 'good' people of either sex and would never hold back any woman volunteer with ability and interest merely because of her sex!" In general, Canadian researchers have found that all issues of equity such as those related to francophones, regional disparities, socioeconomic privilege, ethnicity, athletes' rights, or gender are basically ignored in sport organisations (Macintosh & Whitson, 1990).

In our research we encountered instances of apathy, antagonism, and sometimes outright hostility. None of this came from Sport Canada, which was enormously supportive of our efforts, but from individuals within the organisations we studied. It took the form of refusing to be interviewed, declining to return our questionnaire (59 percent of the men and 28 percent of the women refused), or, if they did reply, taking the opportunity to tell us precisely what they thought of this sort of research. There were also clearly expressed antifeminist sentiments. For example, only 6.5 percent of men, compared to 22 percent of women, agreed that their sport organisation needed more feminists. Indeed, more than one woman told us that being labeled a feminist also meant being labeled a lesbian, which then provided further evidence to exclude these particular women from the organisation. There is a double standard here in that known or assumed lesbians often are not hired in coaching or administrative positions, whereas men with a history of sexual harassment or involvement with female athletes often are. We interpreted much of this hostility to our research as a reflection of very real struggles among men and women over who will have power and who will control, and as a result our study aroused considerable emotion and tension.

Other academic researchers have experienced similar problems, but rarely are there concrete accounts of tensions between the academics who conduct gender equity research and the organisations that fund and use it. A colleague in Australia has done precisely this through an account of his experience with the Australian Sports Commission, the federal authority responsible for amateur sport in Australia. Jim McKay (1993), who teaches in the Department of Sociology and Anthropology at the University of Queensland, received a research grant in 1991 from the Australian Sports Commission to "identify why there were so few women administrators in sporting organisations, with specific emphasis on the barriers to women's access and advancement" (p. 224). In fact, he consulted with me and my colleagues, and his project replicated and extended our study as well as similar work in Britain, Scandinavia, and the United States. He also found that men's and women's perceptions of their sport organisations were highly polarized:

> Whereas most men perceived their organisations to be gender-neutral and governed by merit, most women believed that they were systematically disadvantaged by the following factors: sexual harassment; physical intimidation; having to balance work and family responsibilities; informal male networks; patronage; masculine biases in recruitment, interviewing, selection, development and promotion; inadequate grievance procedures; gender stereotyping; glass ceilings; lack of women role models and mentors; exclusion and isolation; lesbian-baiting; executive inaction regarding GE [gender equity] issues; and the particularly masculine ambiance of sport. (p. 227-228)

None of this came as a surprise to us in that similar studies have found that women must function in organisational cultures in which they are devalued, isolated, and excluded. However, what was unique about Jim McKay's study was that the funding body for his research, the Australian Sports Commission, was the target of unsolicited negative criticism from the respondents in his study as to its handling of gender equity. In his report to the Commission, entitled *Why So Few? Women Executives in Australian Sport*, McKay included a sample of these negative comments, and recommended that "the Commission should have important educative, funding and steering functions in ensuring that GE principles were comprehensively integrated into its own organisation and all ASC-funded organisations" (1993, pp. 226-227). What happened subsequently is a disturbing story of how the Commission questioned respondents' perceptions especially if they were female, required

McKay to make changes in the report, and eventually released an "improved," revised version. The Australian media played a crucial role in affirming the Commission's concerns by claiming that there was no evidence to support the researcher's conclusions and "highly emotive" tone. The lesson to be drawn from McKay's account, and one which he suggests himself, is that attempting to criticize the very body that funds the research often produces a response that is a "sober reminder of some men's formidable capacity to contain and resist women's experiences of gender" (p. 233).

The experience of Jim McKay, and no doubt others, points to the very real tensions and conflicts that praxis-oriented researchers often must face yet never satisfactorily resolve.[10] Organisations, especially if they are funding the research project, usually want researchers to confirm the logic of their policies; and they rarely want to confront the important difference between what they want and what they need. Organisational members and leaders are also often highly antagonistic to theory, which is one side of the praxis coin, the other being action. On the other hand, academics, especially those on promotion and tenure committees, do not value policy-oriented research, so there is little motivation for scholars to engage in it. In sum, policy- or praxis-oriented research is often a "lose-lose" situation for the researcher.

The third example, also from Australia, is a more positive example of the attempt to link theory and practice by means of cultural policy interventions. David Rowe and Peter Brown (1994) of the University of Newcastle describe their role in a community-based research project designed principally to encourage teenage girls to engage voluntarily in sport by improving local media coverage and developing the media and public relations skills of local sporting clubs and associations. The Hunter Medialink Project was funded by the Australian Sports Commission (the same body discussed in the preceding example) through their Aussie/Youth Sports Pilot Demonstration Programme, and it involved six selected sporting associations: field hockey, gymnastics, athletics [track and field], basketball, netball, and surf lifesaving. The rationale for the project was that the enhancement of positive media portrayals of female athletes would encourage teenage girls and women to participate in sport in the Hunter Region, a large coastal area around Newcastle in New South Wales. Its overall approach was one of community-based education and action dedicated to the forging of links between the local media and the selected sporting associations. Workshops on developing media liaison skills were held, resources prepared, and the sporting organisations surveyed and advised on the techniques of seeking and maintaining regular media coverage in order to promote their sports. The role of the researchers was to assess the effectiveness of the Hunter Medialink Project by measuring any increase and improvement in media coverage of women's sport and also any increase in the number of female registrations in the selected sports. In both cases there was modest growth, but as the authors caution, "It is not possible to disentangle the Project from other factors."

The most interesting aspect of the Rowe and Brown study is their observations and reflections about the role of academic researchers in policy-oriented research.[11] Their first point is that policy research, such as the Hunter Medialink Project, imposes real constraints on intellectual and political practice. For instance, the acceptance of external research funding (usually from the state) requires the observation of binding grant conditions that leave little room for flexibility and serendipity. Specific performance criteria and the expectations of the funding body sometimes mean that academic rigor around, for example, validity, reliability, and replicability of findings is breached. Final reports often must be approved for release, which delays the dissemination of information (in Canada they must be also translated into French or English depending on the language of the researcher). If the report is not approved by the funding body, significant modifications may be required (as was the case with Jim McKay's study discussed previously).

Rowe and Brown (1994) also recognize that all research need not, indeed cannot, equally combine theoretical, empirical, and policy discourses. For sure, "attempting a theory-policy-practice synthesis in each project would unduly limit the scope of research" (p. 108). However, they do say the following:

> The attraction of research requiring a policy intervention in sport or any other domain of culture lies principally in its predisposition to "action." Seeking to frame, influence and implement institutional policy . . . helps meet the needs of those politically engaged in the task of seeking equity, as well as the demands of the state and other likely funding bodies for tangible measures of performance and progress. While such activity may produce both useful data and practical results, it does not constitute a research blueprint. Conducting research which requires (in broad terms) policy intervention does not only provide the university-based researchers in sport and leisure with an often unaccustomed task orientation, but also helps to break the circle and rhythm of academic discourse, with its well established network of journals, conferences and peer reviews. Venturing onto the "frontline" does not only advance the cause of equity in sport and leisure, but also highlights new and unanticipated avenues of research. The benefits of policy intervention research lie, therefore, as much in the research *process* as in its explicit *outcomes*. (p. 108-109)

As difficult as it is to do, I would also argue that there is much praxis- or policy-oriented research left to be done in women's sport. For example, far more attention needs to be paid to issues of sexuality: lesbianism and homophobia, sexual harassment and abuse, and sexual violence in sport. Although there is now useful social commentary, increasingly good scholarship, and encouraging policy initiatives around these areas of sexuality,[12] little of this work takes into account the fact that organisations (including sport organisations) not only construct sexuality but are themselves constructed by sexuality. British sociologists Jeff Hearn and Wendy Parkin (1987) coined the term "organisational sexuality" to describe the process whereby organisational life and sexuality occur simultaneously:

> Not only do organisations construct sexuality, as does sexuality construct organisations, but more importantly, the very occurrence of "organisation" invokes "sexuality," and the very occurrence of "sexuality" in the public domain at least, frequently invokes "organisations," so they are no longer separable. (p. 132)

My colleagues and I utilized this notion when attempting to make sense of the gender structure of Canadian national sport organisations (M.A. Hall et al., 1989). What we were trying to understand (and explain) was the structuring of these organisations—more specifically their organisational processes and dynamics—around gender, and this must include sexuality. The concept of sexuality refers not just to individual desire and erotic pleasure, but also to a whole set of social relations that surround physical, bodily desires, both real and imagined. Sexuality is also an issue of power and is often subjugated to the demands and powers of organisations. For example, in the sport organisations we studied, there was a clear valuation of men over women, the public over the private realm, production over reproduction, and heterosexuality over other sexualities, just as there is in other rationalized bureaucracies. However, as Hearn and Parkin (1987) also point out, sexuality has a power or potential power of its own. It can be used to resist the power or powers of the organisation, such as the use of seduction to undermine authority, or it can be used by the powerful in an organisation to counter resistance, such as the tightening up of procedures for appointing female coaches with certain "sexual tendencies." Therefore, the gender structure of organisations, including sport organisations, is characterized by power relations; and these relations control sexuality in different ways. Relations of power are maintained, reinforced, and indeed contested through the processes of organisational sexuality. We need to analyze these processes if we are ever to understand, explain, and eventually alter the gender structure of these organisations. Much of the current work on sport and sexuality, particularly issues of lesbianism, homophobia, and sexual harassment, sometimes fails to appreciate that these issues must be analyzed as the problems of sport institutions and organisations and not those of aberrant individuals. Researchers with a solid understanding of the potential, problems, and limitations of praxis-oriented research could be very helpful here, as in other areas of women's sport, which in many respects is the topic of the next chapter.

Notes

1. For a good overview of this literature, see Wylie, Okruhlik, Morton, and Thielen-Wilson (1990). See also Stanley and Wise (1990), which contains an extended bibliography, Reinharz (1992), which provides a wealth of information on the topic, and Maynard and Purvis (1994), especially chapter 1.

2. The generally accepted epistemological assumptions of foundationalism include: (a) Reality has an objective structure or nature unaffected by or independent of either human understandings of or perspectives on it; (b) the structure or nature of reality in principle is accessible to human understanding or knowledge (objectivism); (c) humans approach the task of gaining knowledge of the world as solitary individuals rather than as socially constituted members of historically changing groups; (d) the principle human faculty for attaining knowledge of reality is reason (rationalism), sometimes working in conjunction with the senses (empiricism); (e) the faculties of reason and sensation are potentially the same for all human beings regardless of their culture, class, race, or sex (universalism) (Jaggar & Bordo, 1989, p. 3).

3. I have borrowed the term "interpretationalism" from Sandra Harding (1990).

4. For an explanation of postmodernism and poststructuralism, see note 5 at the end of chapter 4.

5. See Harding (1986, 1987, 1990, 1991, 1993), as well as Harding and Hintikka (1993).

6. Instead of the notion of standpoint, some feminist philosophers prefer that of "positionality" because, given the differences in women's experiences and realities, the possibility of a single feminist standpoint is both remote and suspect (Code, 1991). It would also presuppose an artificial unity in diversity.

7. I am focusing here on social research and not other forms of research, for example historiography or literary criticism, because it is my area of expertise. Also, the debates within feminist social research tend to be less abstract than those among feminists utilizing postmodernism and deconstructionism.

8. See Lenskyj (1994, pp. 24-26) for a summary of the little research in this area.

9. For a useful resource on feminist action research, which also contains many examples from sport, see Kirby and McKenna (1989). However, although their book details the essentials of how to conduct your own research, they devote only a few paragraphs to "moving from research to action."

10. I am grateful to Jim McKay for the ideas in this paragraph, which he provided after he had read what I had written about his own research experiences.

11. In fact, the write-up of their study was framed as a response to my (M.A. Hall, 1993) lament that the advancement of women and sport has been hamstrung by a largely absent linkage between theory and practice and by the reluctance of theorists to spend time on the front line of women's sport.

12. On issues of homophobia and lesbianism, see the work of Pat Griffin (1992, 1993, 1994; Griffin & Genasci, 1990) in the United States and Helen Lenskyj (1991a) in Canada. For an Australian contribution to the growing body of literature on heterosexism and homophobia in women's sport, see Burroughs, Ashburn, and Seebohm, 1995. There is also some interesting British and American work on the experiences of lesbian physical education students and teachers (Clarke, 1993, 1994; Sparkes, 1994; Sparkes & Tiihonen, 1993; Woods, 1992), as well as Birgit Palzkill's (1990) study of the development of a lesbian identity among German women athletes. See also the excellent teaching video entitled *Out for a change: Addressing homophobia in women's sports*, (1994) produced by Dee Mosbacher which comes with an accompanying curriculum guide prepared by Pat Griffin. The video is available from Woman Vision Productions, 3145 Geary Boulevard, P.O. Box 421, San Francisco, CA 94118. Women's sport advocacy groups like the Canadian Association for the Advancement of Women and Sport and Physical Activity have developed useful background papers and policy initiatives around the issue of sexual harassment (cf. Lenskyj, 1992a, 1992b; CAAWS, 1993). Sport sociologist Don Sabo in the United States, who is also a member of the Board of Trustees of the Women's Sports Foundation, has initiated a research network of academics and others working in this area. In England, Celia Brackenridge is conducting important research on child sexual abuse in sport organizations (Brackenridge, 1994). Finally, see M.B. Nelson (1994) for a useful journalistic account of many of these issues, including the relationship of sport and sexual violence.

From Liberal Activism to Radical Cultural Struggle

6 The development of a radical theoretical critique of sport, and specifically of gender relations, has not seen a parallel in sport activism. Feminist activism in sport has been predominantly "liberal" in nature with the primary focus on ensuring girls and women equal access to sport and recreation opportunities long available to boys and men. The reasons for this are complex. The structure of amateur sport in many Western countries is highly state-subsidized and not likely to produce individuals with a radical critique willing to bite the hand that feeds them. Most sports have an authoritarian power structure that demands discipline and obedience, and works against political awareness—in short, you do what the system or the coach says. At the same time, there has been little support from the grassroots women's movement because politically engaged feminists tend to marginalize or dismiss sport as unimportant to the real struggles over sexual equality. In an article discussing the complete lack of sympathy and support among feminists on an American campus over recent struggles to ensure gender equity in athletics, Julie Phillips (1995) suggests: "Women's sports fit neither their ideological nor their immediate goals. Their idea of organizing was not choosing sides, donning uniforms, scoring points. From them came silence" (p. 32). Sport and feminism are seen as incompatible, and sport is often overlooked, or at best underestimated, as a site of cultural struggle where gender relations are reproduced and sometimes resisted.

The problem, therefore, is that there is a noticeable gap between theory and practice, and minimal analysis about *how* to make women's sport political. In this chapter I address two central questions: First, why is there a gap between theory and practice in women's sport, and second, what can (or should) we do about it? I will show how and why feminist activism around sport has been almost exclusively liberal in philosophy and strategy. Attempts to push the agenda to a more "radical" feminist approach have not met with much success. However, the scholarship about gender (and sport) is becoming increasingly more radical in its critique; yet little of this research is actually used (or read I assume) by those working towards sex equality and gender equity in sport. Perhaps the theory is becoming less accessible, the language more obtuse. In the previous chapter I addressed the issue from the perspective of the researcher and suggested that more researchers needed to venture onto the "front line" of women's sport advocacy by engaging in policy-oriented research, in other words, paying more attention to praxis. In this chapter I examine the issue from the outlook of feminist activists in sport.

Liberal and Radical Feminist Agendas in Sport

Over the past decade there has been a subtle shift in the discourse of human rights in many Western countries from "equality" to "equity." This has occurred in most areas of organizational life, including sport. Equality gener-ally meant "equality of opportunity," and women and other disadvantaged peoples were identified as target groups. In sport, equal opportunity programs were designed to increase women's overall participation by providing them with equal access. The shift to equity signals a more comprehensive view in which the focus is no longer exclusively on women (or any other group) but on a system, in this case sport, that needs to change to accommodate them.[1] As longtime Canadian sport activist Bruce Kidd puts it, "Equality focuses on creating the same starting line for everyone; equity has the goal of providing everyone with the same finish line" (CAAWS, 1993, p. 4). Or, as a United States publication announced, "An athletics program is gender equitable when the men's program would be pleased to accept as its own the overall participation, opportunities and resources currently allocated to the women's program and vice versa" (*Athletics Administration*, April 1993, p. 22).

Whether the focus is on equality or equity, the fundamental philosophy underlying both is best described as liberal reformism. Sport feminists have worked hard, especially over the last decade, to ensure that more sports are now more accessible to more women than ever before. They have fought for, and sometimes won, "easier access and better facilities for women in sports, improved funding and rewards, equal rights with men under the law, top quality coaching on par with men, and an equivalent voice with men in decision-making" (Jennifer Hargreaves, 1994, p. 27).

While liberal approaches to sport equity often seek to provide girls and women with the same opportunities and resources as boys and men, and to remove the barriers and constraints to their participation, they do not always see as problematic the fundamental nature of male-defined sport with its emphasis on hierarchy, competitiveness, and aggression. Liberal feminism in sport also tends to treat women as a homogeneous category without recognizing that there are enormous differences among us in background, class, race, ethnicity, age, disability, and sexual preference that lead to very different expectations and experiences of sport.

A more radical feminist approach[2] adopts an unequivocal women-centred perspective that recognizes and celebrates differences among women and at the same time seriously questions male-dominated and male-defined sport. Women involved in sport advocacy work often fail to take up issues raised by their more radical feminist counterparts outside sport such as sexual harassment and abuse, male violence against women, lesbian visibility, and the politics of difference.

In practice, radical feminists in sport have, as Lenskyj (1991b) suggests, "worked towards establishing autonomous clubs and leagues that are completely outside state-controlled amateur sport systems" (p. 132). These include the many women-only clubs and leagues, some openly lesbian or lesbian-positive, that are free to modify the rules and organize their play along explicitly feminist principles of participation, recreation, fun, and friendship. Examples in Canada include the Notso Amazon Softball League in Toronto and an informal outdoor group in Edmonton called Women of Outdoor Pleasure. More formalized groups offering wilderness and outdoor programs for women, including Woodswomen in the United States and Wild Women Expeditions in Canada, allow participants to define and shape for themselves their experience in the natural environment. In Britain, Jennifer Hargreaves (1994, pp. 250-251) describes a netball[3] club called Queens of the Castle, which is situated in an inner-urban area of London with a predominantly working-class and black membership. Defying the straitlaced, schoolgirl image of British netball, the Queens of the Castle have created their own sport culture by encouraging nonconformist and flamboyant playing clothes, the open discussion and negotiation of all values and practices, a truly caring ethos and support network, and opposition to all forms of racial harassment. They have become successful at attracting young, urban, working-class women to a sport not noted for its egalitarianism. In an often cited study of a women's recreational softball league in the United States, Birrell and Richter (1987) describe how a group of feminists tried to transform their sport by making it more process-oriented, collective, inclusive, supportive, and infused with an ethic of care. There are doubtless many more feminist sporting groups and experiments, and it is surprising how little research has been done to bring them to the fore.

Feminist Activism in Sport: The Canadian Case

Canada is a good case study in how feminist activism in sport has actually worked.[4] It is also the situation with which I am most familiar. The structure of the amateur sport system in Canada—primarily state-funded through national sport bodies—has in large measure been responsible for the liberal path that most feminist organizing has taken. Helen Lenskyj (1991b) also argues that "given the tightly structured, hierarchical nature of Canadian sport systems, there are limited points of entry for feminist activists" (p. 131). The male sport community is the most vocal exponent of sport as a political-neutral activity, and the high degree of government involvement in sport makes it difficult to criticize. The federal government alone invests over $75 million annually in sport for several important reasons: Sport is part of human nature; sport is part of our national identity and an expression of our culture; sport is about pursuing excellence; sport is healthy; and sport is a means to ensure certain social benefits such as bilingualism, gender equity, regional access, and ethical conduct (Fitness and Amateur Sport, 1988). Since the passage of Bill C-131, An Act to Encourage Fitness and Amateur Sport, over 30 years ago, the direct and ongoing intervention of the state has resulted in the rationalisation of the Canadian sport system creating a professional bureaucracy with a more corporate style of management. The control of amateur sport has been largely removed from the hands of volunteers and is now directed by a new professional elite.

There have been primarily three points of entry for feminist activists in Canadian sport: lobbying government, legal challenges, and creating an advocacy organization.

Pressing for Change: Lobbying Government

From the time Bill C-131 was passed in 1961 until the publication of the *Report of the Royal Commission on the Status of Women* in 1970 (which also marked the beginning of institutionalized feminism in Canada) governments at all levels paid little attention to the plight of women's sport. There were two specific recommendations in the report directed at the lack of equal opportunity for girls in school sport programs.[5] The federal government responded (none too willingly) to these recommendations by hiring a women's consultant within Fitness and Amateur Sport whose duties included, among other things, "defining the problems facing women in sport, and establishing programs to alleviate these problems" (M.A. Hall and Richardson, 1982, p. 85). There was continual and strong resistance to the suggestion that the administration of Canadian sport should be restructured to accommodate the needs of women. Feminist sport activists soon realized that their demands attacked the system at its core and that the male-privileged structure would not be challenged easily.

There were, however, some successes throughout the years due to the perseverance of a small number of women located in government, in universities, and in national sport organizations. They include:

1974, 1980	National conferences on women in sport, both of which helped to focus the issues, provide a measure of progress, and mobilize action among various sectors of the sport system
1980	Establishment of the Women's Program in Fitness and Amateur Sport with a mandate and budget, which meant that the federal government was willing to commit some resources and personnel to the issues of women in sport and to encourage national sport organizations to do the same
1981	Founding of a national advocacy organization, the Canadian Association for the Advancement of Women and Sport (CAAWS); the work of this group is discussed later in the chapter
1982	Publication of *Fair Ball: Towards Sex Equality in Canadian Sport* by the Canadian Advisory Council on the Status of Women; this provided a wider audience for discussion of the issues
1986	Publication of *Sport Canada Policy on Women in Sport*, which set out the official goal of equality of opportunity for women at all levels of the sport system
1987	Establishment of the National Coaching School for Women, an annual week-long residential school that operates on explicitly feminist principles and is supported by various partnerships of national sport organizations
1993	Incorporation of gender equity into the guiding principles of the Canadian Sport Council, the collective voice of Canada's sport community

Despite these achievements, a 1992 federal Minister's Task Force on Federal Sport Policy came to the conclusion that, even with an advocacy organization, a federal equity policy, and staffing guidelines to encourage fuller participation by women, little change had occurred over the past 10 years. It was also the view of the task force that the pace of involving and advancing girls and women across the sport continuum and in all levels of sport organizations must be significantly accelerated in order to display fair and equitable treatment of 50 percent of the Canadian population. The authors of *Sport: The Way Ahead* (1992) admonished the sport community: "In accountability for public funding, national sport organizations must understand the legal definition and intent of gender equity and implement it through legislation, constitutions and policies. NSOs must work toward equality by removing systemic barriers and discrimination" (p. 151).

Legal Challenges to Inequality:
The Separate-Versus-Integrated Debates

Until the institution of provincial human rights commissions in the mid-1970s, there was little or no recourse for Canadian girls and women who complained of sex discrimination in sport. Over 17 years have passed since the first sport-related complaints of sex discrimination were filed, and the majority of cases involve girls wishing to play on exclusively male soccer, softball, or ice hockey teams. Other complaints have been directed at the restriction of women playing at private golf clubs during prime hours; pregnancy testing and the reduction of funding to high-performance athletes because of pregnancy; allowing female reporters in male team locker rooms; and, in one case, employment discrimination against a male physical education teacher wishing to teach girls' physical education. The majority of complaints are resolved without going to a formal board of inquiry (or tribunal) or eventually to the courts. In fact, there have been only 12 such formal cases altogether.[6]

The most famous of these cases is that of Justine Blainey, who in 1985 was chosen to play on a boys' ice hockey team in the Metro Toronto Hockey League but was barred from playing by the Ontario Hockey Association. She wanted to play boys' hockey because of the permitted body checking and slap shot, neither of which were allowed in the girls' league. The Blainey case is important because legally it helped strike down a discriminatory clause in the Ontario Human Rights Code that specifically exempted membership in athletic organizations, participation in athletic activities, and access to the services and facilities of recreational clubs from its sex equality provisions.[7]

The Blainey saga is also important because it helped focus debate around an issue that has forever split the women's sport community: sex-separated versus sex-integrated sports and organizations. On one side of the debate are those who argue that only through separate (but equal) programs for girls and boys will equality be achieved and that if girls are allowed to play on boys' teams, then so must boys be allowed to play on girls' teams, which would, in their view, be extremely harmful to girls' and women's sport. The integrationists, on the other hand, argue either that ability and not sex should be the criterion for forming athletic teams, or that where girls do not have the opportunity to participate in a particular sport except through an all-male team or league, they should be permitted to play with boys if they have the necessary skills. They also argue that the "disadvantaged" individual (in this case girls) should be allowed to move up to boys' competition; whereas boys, who are considered "advantaged" should not be allowed to move down. Finally, they argue that because resources are often not available for a parallel girls' structure, one league would be more efficient and less costly.

In Canada, and primarily in the province of Ontario, ice hockey has been the main battleground on which the complexity of these debates has become evident. Although most feminists saw the Blainey case as a victory for human rights, there were some women who argued vehemently against her right to play boys' hockey, notably those involved with girls' and women's hockey. They did so for two reasons: to assure the maintenance of separate-but-equal hockey for girls, and to ensure the legitimacy and recognition of *women's* sport. They argued that the admission of girls to boys' hockey would spell the end of girls' hockey. In fact, they were wrong because "female hockey" has grown tremendously in the last decade both at the recreational and highly competitive levels (and there have been no legions of boys clamouring to play in girls' leagues). They rejected the assertion that the developmental and competitive needs of girls and women cannot be met within their own programs, and they challenged the notion that boys' hockey is a better and more legitimate version of their own game (Theberge, 1995). The women's game does not permit intentional body checking and there is virtually no fighting, both of which are the mainstay of the men's professional game, although there are boys' minor hockey programs and men's recreational leagues that ban them too. Women's hockey and ringette[8] (which is played almost exclusively by girls and women) are good examples of sports that are kept fervently separate by their leaders and organizers because they believe the real question is not the ability of females to play with males, but the legitimacy and recognition of women's sports.

The real test of legal challenges to inequality in sport and recreation is whether they result in a desired effect. Presumably, the desired effect here is to change the ways in which organized sports continue to legitimate male dominance. Certainly in Canada the existence of human rights commissions at both the provincial and federal levels of government has provided a mechanism through which to act on sport-related sex discrimination complaints. Granted, the investigation and litigation of these complaints often takes so long that those who complain are unable to reap the benefits of a positive resolution. For instance, the Blainey case mentioned earlier took nearly three years to resolve, and her lawyer went to court five times. Nevertheless, her case set a precedent, and it has deterred sports clubs and organizations from attempting to exclude girls from boys' sports programs.

Sometimes the mere threat of legal action based on human rights legislation has been sufficient to bring about a change in policy. This was true in the case of an internationally ranked athlete who was denied full financial assistance because of pregnancy, whereas had she been injured, the assistance would have continued. When she filed a complaint with the Canadian Human Rights Commission, the situation was resolved informally, and the Sport Canada policy changed. As in this case, perhaps the most beneficial aspect of legal action is the media attention and public discourse that follows, which serves to increase awareness and to educate the public, both of which are difficult to assess.   *Media Pos!*

Women's Sport Advocacy: CAAWS

CAAWS is the acronym for the Canadian Association for the Advancement of Women and Sport and Physical Activity. The association was founded in 1981 at a workshop funded by the Women's Program in Fitness and Amateur Sport that was attended by a small group of sport administrators, federal government representatives, athletes, coaches, university-based physical educators, and representatives from the major national feminist organizations.

From the beginning, CAAWS saw itself as a feminist organization. Its first mission statement read: "CAAWS seeks to advance the position of women by defining, promoting and supporting a feminist perspective on sport and to improve the status of women in sport." The fact that CAAWS was both openly feminist and government-funded was not unusual given the politics of the state and the Canadian women's movement at the time. As Canadian political scientist Jill Vickers (1992) points out, an operational code of the second-wave women's movement in Canada is the belief that change is possible and that state action is an acceptable way of achieving it. "Most Canadian feminists," she argues, "perceive the state more as a provider of services, including the service of regulation, than a reinforcer of patriarchal norms, and most seem to believe that services, whether child care or medicare, will help" (pp. 44-45). The founders of CAAWS and its subsequent leaders struggled to define its relationship with the larger Canadian women's movement and with the feminist perspective that was the basis of its organizational philosophy. Also, the women's sport network in Canada is relatively small, which has meant that a few key individuals, all with a strong sense of feminism, have remained influential in CAAWS since its inception or have returned at various points to provide leadership and energy.

CAAWS is one of several organizations around the world established in the last 20 years to advocate on behalf of sportswomen. The Women's Sports Foundation in the United States (founded in 1974), the Women's Sports Foundation in the United Kingdom (founded in 1985), Womensport Australia (founded in 1991), and Womensport International (founded in 1994) are examples of these relatively new organizations. Most have evolved quite differently given the unique features of the sport systems in their respective countries, but what they have in common is the goal of providing an alternative to traditional sport organizations. It is imperative, in my view, to study these organizations, reconstruct their organizational histories, examine the ways in which they negotiate their place within the broader sport systems, and assess the extent to which they have been able to maintain their political and advocacy functions.[9]

What is interesting about CAAWS is that it has now drifted away from its original feminist mission. There is no mention of feminism in its latest promotional material, and in 1992 a new vision for the organization was created. Why this happened is difficult to infer, but I suspect that the current leadership is very much aware of the feminist backlash and is unwilling to associate too closely with the dreaded "f" word. Their mission statement now reads: "To ensure that girls and women in sport and physical activity have access to a complete range of opportunities and choices and have equity as participants and leaders." The new vision includes being recognized as the leading organization for girls and women in sport and physical activity in Canada; being inclusive and equitable in its philosophies and practice; providing expert advice, positive solutions, and support to Canada's communities; and operating with efficient and effective management and a strong base of volunteers.

In 1990 CAAWS was one of several national women's organizations in Canada to lose all funding from its major sponsor, the Secretary of State Women's Program, and although it had some project money from the Women's Program in Sport Canada, it was forced to downsize drastically and rely on volunteer assistance. The organization struggled to survive only to be saved a year later by an agreement to move it into the mainstream of sport by establishing an office in the Canadian Sport, Fitness, and Administration Centre in Ottawa, where all national and multisport organizations are located, and to provide it with substantial core and project funding through the Women's Program in Sport Canada.[10]

There is an important distinction to be made here between an organization that promotes *sport for women* and one that advocates for *women in sport*. The former denotes a more radical feminist perspective in the sense that CAAWS is a women's organization that promotes its aims through sport; the latter represents a distinctly liberal approach that seeks to improve the lot of women already in sport through a sport organization for women. As an organization, CAAWS has struggled between these two visions for its entire existence. Its current focus on gender equity, its physical presence at the Canadian Sport, Fitness, and Administration Centre, its visibility and work in the Canadian Sport Council, and its willingness to work with other national sport organizations means that its path is more decidedly liberal now than ever before.

Even though organizations like CAAWS are expressly liberal feminist, there are still struggles within them about differing ideological positions. The primary difference has been between those who proclaim a liberal approach versus those who seek a more radical feminist approach, and, for the most part, the struggle has revolved around sexual politics. Throughout its existence, CAAWS has made a serious effort to be both antihomophobic and lesbian-positive. In the mid-1980s, the following resolutions were passed at various annual general meetings: "CAAWS endorses the inclusion of sexual orientation in the Canadian Human Rights Code"; "CAAWS is opposed to discrimination against lesbians in sport and physical activity, and that CAAWS undertakes to support advocacy efforts to ensure lesbian equality of rights"; and "Given that there are lesbians within CAAWS, and homophobia within CAAWS, the Association needs to address these internal concerns." However, despite these well-meaning resolutions and the workshops that produced them, lesbians in CAAWS have experienced difficulty in keeping the lesbian visibility and homophobia issues on the agenda. The membership and leadership have always been split between those who see sexuality as a private and personal concern versus those who see it as a political issue. For some, the organization was perceived to have an "image problem," as expressed through letters of concern to the CAAWS newsletter, whenever the lesbians in CAAWS became too visible. For others, and certainly for those taking a more radical stance, the human rights and education strategies were insufficient because they were too liberal and they depoliticized sexuality. There has been relative silence on the issue for the past few years, and to some extent the state has played a role in enforcing this silence with the 1987 directive from the Secretary of State Women's Program (which was at the time a major source of funding for CAAWS) that it would no longer fund proposals and groups whose primary purpose was "to promote a view on sexual orientation."[11]

CAAWS now sees itself more as part of the Canadian sport community and much less as a feminist organization linked to the women's movement. This "new vision" is reflected in its goals for 1993-94: gender equity and leadership, research, communication, partnership and liaison, and community initiatives. To meet these goals, CAAWS develops educational materials (e.g., *Towards Gender Equity for Women in Sport: A Handbook for National Sport Organizations*); provides consultation and hands-on support to sport organizations; designs seminars and workshops; publishes research reports (available studies include female participation rates in major games, self-esteem and sport, sexual harassment, gender equity and the law, girls on boys' teams, eating disorders and sport, and pay equity and sport); publishes a regular newsletter, *Action Bulletin*; hosts the annual Breakthrough Awards honouring individuals and organizations; handles increasing media inquiries; and liaises regularly with relevant organizations and groups, as well as many other activities.

CAAWS is governed by an elected board of directors comprising about 10 individuals who represent the various provinces or regions of Canada. The geographical size of Canada makes it expensive for the board to meet in one place, so a smaller executive committee really runs the organization in conjunction with the paid executive director who, along with one or two staff, is situated in an office in Ottawa. Membership in the organization has been small at the best of times (around 200), and at present there is no membership fee—one simply gets on a mailing list, which now comprises some 2,500 individuals and groups.

Within their internal structures, organizations like CAAWS have not paid much attention to the feminist process and tools that have been issues in other women's groups. By feminist process, what is usually meant is a more caring and nurturing environment involving consensus decision-making, rotating leadership positions, and particular tools used during meetings such as time keepers, vibes watchers, and note takers. For a specific period, between 1987 and 1989, the CAAWS board of directors experimented with these processes and others in an attempt to make themselves more cognizant of their feminist roots. However, like most groups, they discovered that these efforts took considerable time and demanded commitment and that they were often resisted by those who were more task-oriented and wished "to get some work done." Consequently, and also as a result of increased pressure from their funding sources to become more professionalized, they abandoned their attempts to utilize specific feminist processes.

Is it possible for women's sport advocacy groups like CAAWS, and others around the world, to be "feminist," to see themselves as part of the larger women's movement in their respective countries? To what extent are these organizations "pro-woman" in the sense of improving women's collective status, opportunities, power, and self-esteem, as well as being political and socially transformational (Martin, 1990)? To what extent can they maintain and enhance their political and advocacy functions? At the same time, how do these organizations negotiate their place within the broader sport systems, both at the national and international levels, as they attempt to provide alternatives to traditional sport organizations? Understanding the potential for the politicization of both women's sport and women in sport is crucial.

Politicizing Women's Sport (and Women in Sport): Radical Cultural Struggle

> The politicization of women's sports is unusual. For the most part, sportswomen see sports in an insular way and claim that there is no connection between participation and politics. As a result discrimination goes unchallenged: a deaf ear is turned toward people who make sexist and racist remarks and nothing is done to change the practices of clubs that (often unintentionally) discriminate against certain groups so that they remain marginalized, alienated and powerless. Dominant structures and discourses are exclusionary; they are the

basis of institutionalized discrimination which is hard to shift. There have been few organized initiatives in women's sports which look beyond the struggle for greater equality with men, and which relate the gender dimension to wider social and political issues as a part of the everyday life experiences of participation. (Jennifer Hargreaves, 1994, p. 254)

As Jennifer Hargreaves suggests, and I agree, sportswomen generally have been resistant to taking an overtly political stance on women's issues and on issues of discrimination. The politics and practice of feminism have not always been recognized as particularly important or relevant. By politics we mean the struggle to define and control women's sport: its meanings and values, the structures required, and the debates over policy. Feminist practice in sport, when it does occur, ranges from liberal reformism to a more controversial radicalism and there is inevitable tension between the two approaches. Where governments have made women's sport a priority, their programs and policies have been overwhelmingly liberal but with a welcome shift from a focus on equality to equity over the past decade. When women's sport advocacy groups such as CAAWS in Canada and similar organizations around the world become primarily dependent for funding on either the state or the private sector, they focus more on a liberal gender equity framework for change and are less willing and often resistant to engaging in radical cultural politics. This effectively depoliticizes the issues surrounding women in sport (homophobia is a good example) and makes it difficult for those interested in pursuing more radically defined issues and change to be effective. Male-defined sport can be, and often is, challenged and resisted, but the resistance takes place primarily at the local level far removed from state-controlled amateur sport systems.

The history of modern sport, as in all areas of popular culture, is a history of cultural struggle. There have been numerous and often bitter conflicts in Canada over which sporting practices, styles, beliefs, and bureaucratic forms should predominate. For instance, some traditional sporting practices (e.g., lacrosse) were marginalized or incorporated into more "respectable" and "useful" ways of playing as the colonizers (primarily the British) imposed their particular sports on the colonized. The class-based struggles of the late 19th and early 20th centuries over the meaning of amateurism and its alternative, professionalism, led eventually to the emergence of commercialized sport. Marginalized groups, like women and racial and ethnic minorities, have struggled to preserve their values and their ways of playing. Privileged groups in our society—seemingly by consent—are able to establish their own cultural practices as the most valued and legitimate, whereas subordinate groups (like women) have to fight to gain and maintain control over their own sport experience and at the same time have their alternative practices and activities recognized as legitimate by the dominant sporting culture. Sport in our culture is still viewed by many as a "masculinizing project," a cultural practice where boys learn to be men and male solidarity is forged. Sport remains a prime site for the maintenance of masculine hegemony. It is for this reason that when women actively participate in the symbols, practices, and institutions of sport, what they do there is often not considered "real" sport, nor in some cases are they viewed as real women.[12]

What follows from this notion of sport as a site of cultural struggle is that the history of women in sport is a history of cultural resistance. In fact the very presence of women in the male preserve of sport is evidence of "leaky hegemony" (Birrell & Theberge, 1994b). The Victorian women who ignored medical warnings regarding athletic activity were challenging the primacy of the uterus, and when they rode defiantly about on their "safety bicycles" (ones with rubber tires) in their fashionable bloomers, they broke tradition and asserted their independence. Although the school games and sports girls began to play at the end of the century were intended to make them healthier and so fitter for academic toil and ultimately motherhood, they nonetheless challenged the notion of the "weaker sex." Their new-found physical freedom in the 1920s and 1930s produced great women athletes like Suzanne Lenglen, Helen Wills, "Babe" Didrikson, Gertrude Ederle, "Bobby" Rosenfeld, and so many others who were publicly admired, indeed treated like "personalities," in the new era of women's competitive sport. Yet newly trained women physical educators fought to keep women's sport as unlike men's and as far removed from male control as possible by advocating separate programs, teachers, coaches, and officials. They campaigned against all championships (including the Olympics), tournaments, and interscholastic competitions, branding them "unwholesome." Despite these concerns, women's sport in countries not devastated by the Second World War was able to flourish. However, following the war, men's professional sport and its subsequent dependence on television brought us to where we are today, with less coverage and attention paid to women's sport than was true 50 and 60 years ago. Resistance, therefore, is never wholly successful, and it often does not result in a transformed cultural practice. The point is that sport is an important, though often overlooked or underestimated, site for understanding the reproduction of (and resistance to) gender relations.

There is a long road ahead before any form of radical cultural politics is recognized as being both viable and necessary to future change in women's sport. While writing this chapter I attended an international conference on women's sport organized by the British Sports Council and supported by the International Olympic Committee. At the conference were some 300 delegates from over 85 countries representing governmental and nongovernmental organizations, national Olympic committees, international and national sport federations, and educational and research institutions. The conference specifically addressed the issue of "how to accelerate the process of change that would redress the imbalances women face in their participation and involvement in sport," and it approved a declaration the aim of which was "to develop a sporting culture that enables and values full involvement of women in every aspect of sport."[13] Thematic workshops addressed the continuing problems that plague women's sport: the lack of women in sports administration, development of women coaches, and gender bias in physical education and research. Issues seminars focused on the usual topics: equal opportunity legislation, integration versus separation, cross-cultural differences, challenging sexism, marketing strategies, working in a male environment, and a few more controversial topics such as women's sport in Muslim cultures, sexual harassment, homophobia, and integrating women athletes with disabilities. Skills seminars provided information on mentoring, networking, advocacy and lobbying, community sports leadership, dealing with the media, and gender awareness training. Delegates agreed to establish and develop an International Women in Sport Strategy, which they hope will be endorsed and supported by governmental and nongovernmental organizations involved in sport development on all continents and will enable model programs and successful developments to be shared among nations and sporting federations.

Very few researchers and scholars whose work relates to women and sport attended the conference, which points again to the gap between theory/ research and practice I discussed in chapter 5. Indeed, very little of the research and scholarship readily available was incorporated into the conference program, although several recommendations vaguely addressed the need for more research.

There was general agreement that strong, international women and sport networks are needed for providing mutual support; for exchanging knowledge, skills, and "good practice"; and for sharing resources. A new organization, Womensport International, was announced at the conference. It aspires to be an umbrella group that will seek positive change for girls and women in sport and physical activity by facilitating global networking and communication. Given the fact that the founders of Womensport International wish the organization to be global in scope and outlook and to connect a vast array of differing cultures, it is no wonder that notions of politicization and radical cultural struggle are absent from its vision. However, it must take up this more radical perspective; otherwise, it will become like other liberal-oriented women's sport advocacy associations, which to their credit have made significant gains in bringing more girls and women into sport but have not been effective in challenging the male-dominated and male-defined nature of sport.

Conclusion: Whither the Future?

In the last two chapters I have discussed the separation of academic knowledge from social activism—in chapter 5 from the perspective of feminist research and researchers and in this chapter from the viewpoint of women's sport advocacy organizations. I have identified the noticeable gap between theory and practice in women's sport and have explained why it has occurred and why it continues to be a problem. Clearly we need to move beyond this separation. We need to find ways to connect the two; otherwise, it will take a long time to bring substantial change to the male-defined and male-dominated sports world. In the last few sentences of this book, I cannot offer a master plan to bring about this integration of theory and action, to create a workable feminist praxis in sport, nor do I have many concrete suggestions except what I have presented throughout. I do know, however, that a feminist praxis is badly needed at this stage in our efforts to bring about change, and I offer a few final thoughts and ideas.

First, all of us—students, educators, sportswomen, administrators, and volunteers—must not get rattled because the label "feminism" has yet again become a "dirty" word. We are in a period of significant backlash against feminism fueled by the growing strength of the "new right" with its moral panic over permissiveness, loss of individual freedoms, and "collapse" of family values. I remind the reader that when I began this journey, in my childhood after the war and into the 1950s, feminism was a dirty word then too, and nobody I knew used it. Second-wave feminism, now remarkably complex, sophisticated, and varied after 30 years of scholarship and activism, is neither dead nor about to be buried. It does, however, have its critics and dissenters, many of whom consider themselves feminists. This is a natural evolution for an intellectual and social movement that in the larger scale has not been around very long.

In my office, I keep a postcard that reads: "Post Feminism—keep your bra and burn your brain" to remind me that "postfeminism" is such a ludicrous notion. The idea of postfeminism emanates from several different sources. There are those within feminism who argue that it has achieved its aim and is no longer necessary, and there are those from without who blame feminism for the ills of society such as the rise of single mothers and increasing violence among the young (Scraton, 1994). Postmodernist feminists have also contributed to the debate because of their distrust of "grand" theories, including feminism, and their insistence that the category "woman" is no longer meaningful (Jackson, 1992; Modleski, 1991). Postfeminism, or a feminism without women, simply does not make any sense when I see the pitiful material conditions under which many women live in my own society and more so on a global scale. As Sheila Scraton has argued in her critique of postfeminism in the context of women's leisure,

> Far from being in a post-feminist stage, we are in a period of time in which we need more knowledge of women's leisure in the 1990s, research that acknowledges the continual exploitation and subordination of many women yet is sensitive to a changing world of changing conditions and the current developments within feminist discourse. (p. 258)

I recognize too that women athletes and students of physical education continue to be apprehensive about using the label "feminism" because in some circles claiming to be feminist is tantamount to declaring yourself a lesbian (Griffin, 1992). I agree with Pat Griffin, who works tirelessly to help athletes, students, educators, coaches, administrators, and others to understand that it is empowering *not* to be intimidated by these labels and that there are many alternatives to silence or denial. She and others have also shown how fear about homosexuality has the power to intimidate and discourage all women from participation in sport, certainly those sports seen as the preserve of men.[14] My experience is that students today are willing to discuss these issues, but they need considerable guidance; they also need to know about the many lesbian and gay sport leagues that are flourishing in North America and elsewhere that provide lesbian and gay individuals with an opportunity to openly acknowledge their sexual identities.

I know that for many young women (including most of my students), the world now, and certainly the sports world, is different and more equitable than when I was in their place. Yet I find that these same students have little understanding or appreciation for the struggles women (and other oppressed peoples) have endured to negotiate a fairer and more just place for themselves in this world. My students have little comprehension of the potential for human ''agency''—those individual practices and actions that can transform social systems. At the same time, they find it difficult to recognize, let alone analyze, the structures and processes of the social systems that both enable and constrain them. If they study social change at all, and particularly social movements like feminism, they most likely study *what* gets changed and *when it gets changed*, but not *how* it changes (Messer-Davidow, 1991). Therefore, we need to teach students and others the actual practice of feminist social change, what I have called feminist praxis. We need to offer academic courses that include an action component that will provide practical experience in the praxis of social change—perhaps an internship with a women's sport advocacy group or a gay and lesbian sport league, or assisting with a local ''media watch'' to monitor the coverage and portrayal of women's sport—the possibilities are endless.

I have spoken of the need for more researchers to engage in change-oriented social research. In Canada, as I am sure is true in other countries, there are several groups, some local and some provincial or national, now working toward change for girls and women in sport. There are, for example, On the Move programs in various municipal centres, provincial groups like Promotion Plus in British Columbia and the 52% Solution in Saskatchewan, and at the national level, the Canadian Association for the Advancement of Women and Sport and Physical Activity (discussed earlier). All of these groups are focused on bringing gender equity to sport programs, facilities, resources, and media coverage. These groups and social-change programs need to be studied and evaluated to find out how they work, who benefits, what has been successful, and what changes have been accomplished.

My final point is that we can and should use computer technology to expand our women's sport networks. I have used computers for over 20 years and have observed remarkable changes in their capabilities and power, but I have never seen anything like the recent, rapid expansion of the information highway. The amount of information available through the Internet grows exponentially almost daily, and, perhaps surprisingly, there is already a good deal of information readily available pertaining to women's sport. For example, just as I was finishing this section, someone added a World Wide Web site that contains an enormous amount of useful information pertaining to Title IX in the United States. By the time you are reading this, there will be much more information available on all sorts of topics and issues. Computer bulletin boards, news groups, and electronic mail discussion groups on women's sport, as well as many others about feminism, already exist. I recognize that not everyone has access to this computer technology, especially those without an institutional base or in a country not so technologically advanced, but this too will change. We can use this technology to communicate with each other, share ideas and "good practices," discuss issues, resolve our differences, and evolve our strategies. Cyberspace could be the site of a global feminist praxis in sport.

Notes

1. For a clear and insightful analysis of this shift as it relates to sport, see Jennifer Hargreaves (1994, pp. 237-242). See also Margaret Talbot's (1989) useful analysis of differing interpretations of equality within the sport and physical education context.
2. Theoretically, radical feminism has always placed more analytical primacy on sexuality than on capitalism in explaining women's oppression, and in this sense, it has been accused of essentialism. Politically, radical feminists have stressed the importance of issues around sexuality—sexual harassment, sexual abuse, rape, domestic violence, incest, birth control, abortion, pornography, prostitution, sexual freedom, sexual autonomy, homophobia—and fought for changes to laws and policies. Radical feminists have also worked hard to develop a woman-centred and woman-supporting culture in their communities. Feminist theorists today are not much engaged in the debates around production and reproduction, although in my opinion they still have some value (see M.A. Hall, 1984b). However, there are still many feminist activists who see themselves as "radical" in the sense that the oppression of women is at the *root* of all other oppressions and that women's oppression is based in part on sexual oppression defined not just as sexual relations but as the total process of human reproduction. It is in this sense that I am using the term "radical" here.
3. Netball is a team game, the structure and rules of which are similar to basketball except that court movement, ball handling, and guarding the

basket are more restrictive. With the exception of Canada, it is played extensively throughout the British Commonwealth.

4. This section has been summarized from a much more detailed study (M.A. Hall, 1995b).

5. *Recommendation 77*: We recommend that the provinces and territories (a) review their policies and practices to ensure that school programmes provide girls with equal opportunities with boys to participate in athletic and sports activities, and (b) establish policies and practices that will motivate and encourage girls to engage in athletic and sport activities. *Recommendation 78*: We recommend that, pursuant to section 3(d) of the federal Fitness and Amateur Sport Act, a research project be undertaken to (a) determine why fewer girls than boys participate in sport programmes at the school level and (b) recommend remedial action.

6. For a summary and analysis of these cases, see M.A. Hall and Richardson (1982, pp. 18-28), and Meade (1993).

7. In April 1986, because of an appeal by Blainey, the Ontario Court of Appeal struck down subsection 19(2) of the Ontario Human Rights Code, ruling that it contravened the equality provisions (section 15) in the Canadian Charter of Rights and Freedoms. Blainey then took her original complaint against the Ontario Hockey Association back to an Ontario Board of Inquiry, which eventually ordered that the OHA be prohibited from refusing any female the opportunity to compete for a position on a hockey team on the same basis as males.

8. Ringette is a winter team game designed specifically for girls as a more "feminine" version of ice hockey. It originated in Canada (specifically in northern Ontario) in the 1970s, is now played extensively across the country, and has spread internationally to the United States, Scandinavia, and parts of Europe. It is played on a regulation size hockey rink; players wear skates but play with a doughnut-shaped rubber quoit and wooden stick with no blade. The object is to pass the quoit from player to player until someone is in a position to shoot on the goal.

9. To this end, see M.A. Hall (1995a), plus the growing number of graduate student theses on these organizations.

10. As I was revising this section, the federal government announced, in its latest round of budget cuts, that Sport Canada's budget was substantially reduced, which means much less government support to many sport associations including CAAWS. The government has also seen fit to shut down several status of women programs and will provide much less funding to volunteer sector groups.

11. Similarly in Britain, the 1988 Local Government Act, which introduced Clause 28 prohibiting the promotion of homosexuality using public money, meant that it was extremely difficult for groups like the Women's Sports Foundation to declare openly that it supported lesbianism. Since it now receives substantial funding from the British Sports Council, all public discussions about lesbian visibility have ceased. In the United

States, the Women's Sports Foundation has always been reluctant to deal openly with lesbianism because in the past corporate sponsors have threatened to withdraw funding. For more information on the sexual politics within women's sport advocacy organizations, see M.A. Hall (1995b).

12. Some useful articles that discuss these ideas in more depth are Bryson (1987, 1990), Jennifer Hargreaves (1989), Messner (1988), and I.M. Young (1979).

13. See the Brighton Declaration on Women and Sport, Women Sport and the Challenge of Change International Conference, Brighton, England, May 5-8, 1994.

14. For useful resources in this area, see note 12 in chapter 5.

Index

Empiricism, 11, 71, 77, 86 n. 2
Empowerment. *See* Power
Epistemology, 69, 70-74
Essentialism, 51, 52, 53, 105 n. 2
Ethnicity, and sports, 43-44. *See also* Women of colour
Evans, Sara, 47 n. 9
"Everyday" (ordinary), study of, 36

F

Fair Ball: Towards Sex Equality in Canadian Sport (Canadian Advisory Council on the Status of Women), 93
Fausto-Sterling, Anne, 17
Felshin, Jan, 7
Female Bodybuilders Home Page (Internet), 67 n. 8
Female Eunuch, The (Greer), 2
Feminine Mystique, The (Friedan), 1
" 'Feminine Woman' and an 'Athletic Woman' as Viewed by Female Participants and Non-Participants in Sport, A" (Hall), 5-6
Femininity
and athleticism, 18-21, 51
and beauty culture, 57-58, 60
conception of, 19, 51
and muscular symmetry, 62
reconstruction of ideal, 58
as social construct, 23
stereotypes of, 5-6, 59
technologies of, 54
Feminism. *See also* Feminist theory
and activism, 92-99, 102-105
backlash against, 103
and bodies, 50-65
in Canada, 92
development of, 1
and epistemology, 70-74
and feminist process, 99
French, 24
practice of, 36
resistance to, 8
relevance of, 6-8
second-wave, 2, 4, 8 n. 1, 50, 96, 103
in sport psychology, 23-25
Feminist empiricism, 72

Feminist film theory, 62-63
Feminist postmodernism, 72, 73
Feminist research (scholarship)
definition of, 74-76
as *praxis*, 76-85
Feminist sport psychology practice, 23, 25, 30-31
Feminist standpoint theory, 72-73
Feminist theory. *See also* Feminism
development of, 30-31
and history, 37-40
influence of, 13
influence on Hall, 5, 7
practice of, 29, 36, 102-103, 104
52% Solution, Saskatchewan, 104
Figes, Eva, 2
Fine, Michelle, 24-25
Firestone, Shulamith, 2, 66 n. 2
For the Record (Spender), 8 n. 1
Foucault, Michel, 53-56
Foundationalism, 71, 86 n. 2
Francis, Bev, 60-61
Frank, Arthur W., 49-50
Frank, Blye, 46
Fraser, Nancy, 30, 55
Frauenformen (West German collective), 64
Friedan, Betty, 1
Functionalism, of sex-role theory, 21-23
Fuβballsport als ideologie (Vinnai), 32

G

Gallop, Jane, 66 n. 2
Gatens, Moira, 53, 66 n. 2
Gender (sexual difference)
care/autonomy distinction in, 19
history of, 38-39
influence on social life, 74
neurobiological basis of, 13-18, 40
restructuring of, 42
retention and celebration of, 50, 51
as social/cultural construction, 22, 23, 40-42, 66 n. 2
Western construct of, 19, 51
Gender bias, 7

About the Author

Professor M. Ann Hall is a member of the Faculty of Physical Education and Recreation at the University of Alberta in Canada, where she also has taught and held administrative positions within the Women's Studies Program (which she helped to establish). She received her master's degree from the University of Alberta in 1968 and her PhD in physical education from the University of Birmingham (England) in 1974.

Dr. Hall serves on the editorial board of the *Journal of Sport and Social Issues* and is a member of many professional organizations and feminist groups, including the North American Society for the Sociology of Sport, the Canadian Association for the Advancement of Women in Sport, and the Canadian Women's Studies Association. She has written extensively on the topic of women in sport and has presented at dozens of conferences internationally.

When she can find a few moments for leisure activities, Dr. Hall enjoys horseback riding, skiing, hiking, swimming, and other outdoor pursuits near her cottage in Eastern Canada.